In Search of Unicorns

In Search of
Unicorns

A Guide to the Unicorn Tarot

by
Suzanne Star

Artwork by
Liz Hilton

U.S. Games Systems, Inc.
Publishers
Stamford, CT 06902 USA

Copyright ©1997 by U.S. Games Systems, Inc.

First Edition

Star, Suzanne
  In Search of Unicorns: A Guide to the Unicorn Tarot
Author Suzanne Star/Artwork by Liz Hilton

ISBN 0-88079-198-5

Library of Congress Catalog Card Number: 95-061766

99 10 9 8 7 6 5 4 3

Printed in Canada

U.S. GAMES SYSTEMS, INC.
179 Ludlow Street
Stamford, CT 06902 USA

Table of Contents

The events in this book are based on Suzanne Star's true life experiences.

Chapter 1

In Search of Unicorns

I have always been fascinated by the unknown. For as far back as I can remember, I have read about fairies, goblins, and mythical beasts, but the creature that most intrigued me was the unicorn. Theory has it that every myth is based in reality, somewhere along the line, no matter how remote, and so it was that I became determined to find the truth about unicorns.

I was traveling through the United States of America when the idea for this book first began. High up in the Smoky Mountains, I felt as if I were on the top of the world. The view was breathtakingly spiritual, nothing but rolling mountains for miles and miles, and smoky blue and purple mists gently rising up from the valley below.

On the last day of my visit to the States, I picnicked in a place called Sapphire Valley. It was in this place that something wonderful happened to me. Little did I know then that what was about to follow would change my life forever.

It was midday and the sweltering heat from the sun was beating down on my face. I decided to take shelter from the sun, so I found a cool, green, shady place to sit down. I tried hard to envisage a unicorn coming out of the trees, and wondered what he would be like.

•✦• •✦• •✦•

I began my search for unicorns many years ago. When I was a small child, my grandmother would often sit me on her lap and read me wondrous, magical tales of unicorns, the mystical beasts that looked like wispy horses with a single golden horn in the center of their foreheads.

She told me that men had almost made unicorns extinct many years ago. Hunters would use young girls to lure the unicorns, for they knew that unicorns are attracted by purity and virtue. The poor beast would be trapped and slain, partly for sport, but mainly for the unicorn's horn and its magical properties.

As time went on, I had an overwhelming desire to find this mystical beast. On this particular afternoon, I started remembering all the good times I had enjoyed with my grandma. She was a very wise old lady, blessed with the gift of strong perception. She always gave me the feeling that she knew a lot more than she would actually say. I was amazed how she could tell me about things that were going to happen, and then they would come true, just as she had predicted.

I remembered my grandmother telling me, when I was eleven years old, that if there was any way of coming back to visit me after she had passed away, she would. I never gave it much thought at the time, but then, sadly, she died just before my twelfth birthday. I missed her a great deal. She hadn't come back to visit me, as she promised; and I couldn't help wondering where we all go when we die, if there really was a way back.

Lying on the mountain, I became more deeply engrossed in thinking about my grandmother's unicorn tales. My thoughts were suddenly interrupted by a strange noise. It sounded like very light footsteps. I quickly glanced around. At first I saw nothing, but then I thought I saw a pure, glimmering light in the distance. It appeared to be coming toward me.

Before me stood the most beautiful animal I had ever seen. It was a pure white unicorn with the most sylph-like, wispy body and long slender legs. He stood absolutely still, like a statue. He looked straight into my eyes as if to size me up to see if I was a threat to him. His aura was strong and powerful, his horn glistening gold. On his back was a young woman wearing a flowing, white gown.

The woman's voice softly spoke to me. "I have come to guide you to the magical kingdom of unicorns." I was spellbound. She softly said, "I am the Lady of the Star, and I have come to grant your wish. Follow me!" She turned the unicorn around and headed off in the direction from which she had appeared. I followed eagerly in anticipation of what I was about to experience.

It seemed as though we had been walking for hours when the lady and the unicorn came to a halt. The woman looked at me and smiled. It was a reassuring smile, in the same way that my grandma used to smile at me when I was young. I felt a warm glow inside me as though everything was going to be all right. I felt secure, yet excitement was running through my veins. The Lady of the Star then turned and pointed. She had very dainty elegant hands with long slender fingers. My gaze followed her hand to see where she was leading me.

THE ENCHANTED FOREST

There before me lay an enchanted forest, dark and mysterious; it was a labyrinth, a giant maze of bramble bushes, bracken, and trees. The whole landscape appeared to rise up gently from the plain, until it kissed the golden horizon. In the far distance I saw a spiral path that rose up to a golden-spired fairy tale castle on the top of a hill. Words escaped me. I had never seen anything like it in all my dreams. The woman's soft voice broke my thoughts.

"In order to gain spiritual strength and wisdom, you must first conquer the labyrinth. Then, if you manage to get though that, you must ascend to the higher spiral spiritual path in an anti-clockwise manner in order to reach the top and find what you are really looking for. For Suzanne, you are the chosen one, the 'Babe of the Abyss'!"

I turned to ask her what she meant, if this was the only way – and what was that castle on the pinnacle? But she had vanished; just a few glittering sparkle dust particles remained, falling to the ground like snowflakes.

I paused for a moment, pondering what the Lady of the Star had told me. What did it mean to be the "Babe of the Abyss"? I was soon to find out!

With great determination, I began my quest to find out what lay ahead. I eagerly approached the labyrinth of trees and bramble bushes, but it appeared overgrown and impassable.

I sat down on the ground and looked on in frustration. There just seemed to be no way in. I had already walked a long way and was growing weary and grumpy. Just then, a small insect flashed past my face, and I flicked my hand to shoo it away. The insect hovered over my head. I flicked again but it was too quick for me. With the third flick of my hand, I caught it! While falling to the ground, it seemed to glow. I had thought it was just an overgrown glow-bug until it landed.

I was astonished to see that it was a tiny white horse. I carefully picked it up and lay it in the palm of my hand. There was a glowing white light around him, but he seemed lifeless. As I looked closer I realized that he wasn't a horse at all – he was a tiny unicorn! Part of his horn was missing. I immediately scouted around looking for the little horn, which must have come off when I knocked him down! Sure enough, there it was, lying on the ground, glistening gold.

I remembered from my research into unicorns that men used to slay this mystical beast for its horn and the horn's magical properties and healing abilities. While the unicorn's horn is very powerful for humans, it is also the unicorn's strength and life force. Therefore, if a unicorn is separated from his horn, he will surely die!

I felt really guilty, for if I had not mistaken him for an insect he would still be alive. "Oh, what a fool I am!" I wailed. Then it occurred to me, what if the magical healing properties of this little unicorn horn are so strong that it could actually bring him back to life? "It's worth a try," I thought, and placed the horn on the unicorn's petite head.

At first nothing seemed to happen, and then as if by magic the unicorn started to move. He rose to his feet and shook himself. There he stood in my hand, looking at me as if he wanted to say something. I stroked his tiny head with one finger and apologized for mistaking him for a fly.

He seemed very friendly and rubbed his head on my thumb, and then he took off and flew toward the trees. I watched as the trees parted and made an opening for him. An entrance! Wondering if the entrance was big enough for me to get through, I chased excitedly after the unicorn.

I made it just in time; right after I got through the opening the trees closed up just as they were a moment before. I made it – I was inside the labyrinth, where I found myself in the middle of a pathway that branched out in three different ways.

I was surrounded by trees so dense that I could not see which way was the way to the castle. The little unicorn came and landed on my shoulder. Just then, in a flash of light, a mysterious-looking man appeared. He was a mature man, dressed in a flowing purple gown with a hood that came up over his head.

"Where are you going, Neophyte?" he asked. He had a strange magical aura around him and I must admit I was a little scared, but I replied, "To the castle. Do you know the way?"

"The castle!" he said with a smile on his face. "You mean the enchanted palace! Yes, I know the way," he replied.

"Please, will you tell me," I said rather sheepishly.

"I am the Magician! The way is to follow your feelings, but you must always remember to keep to the right hand path." And with that, he vanished into thin air. I suddenly felt invincible.

"I can do it," I said to myself. I turned to the little unicorn, but he too had disappeared. The Magician must have frightened him away. But I was full of encouragement now.

"Keep to the right hand path," the Magician had said, so I turned to the third path that was on my right hand side and went on my way.

THE VISION IN THE LAKE

I walked for ages over paths that twisted, turned, and merged from time to time, but I always kept to the right. The right-hand path led to a clearing in the trees. This looked like a good place to rest awhile; it seemed so peaceful here. I could hear water trickling in the distance, and as I turned to see from whence it came I saw a silver stream flowing into a small pool. The water looked pure, and I ran toward it for a drink and to freshen up. Kneeling by the edge of the water, I placed both hands in and splashed my face.

As I rubbed my eyes, I looked down and saw a reflection in the water. To my astonishment, I saw a full-size unicorn, white, with a silver horn. He was gently dipping the tip of his horn into the pool, creating ripples that were fanning out across the water. I looked behind me to see him properly, but he was nowhere to be seen. I quickly looked down into the water again, and sure enough, there he was, but this time the unicorn was not alone.

Beside the unicorn a beautiful woman was kneeling down at the water's edge. She looked at me through the silver waters and softly spoke.

"Hello, Suzanne," she said. "I am the High Priestess, and this is my unicorn."

"How do you know my name?"

"I possess great powers of insight. I know everything."

"Why is your unicorn dipping his horn in the water like that?" I inquired.

"He is purifying the waters with his magical horn to make it safe for you to drink." she replied. "Drink some more; the magical properties in the water will help to give you strength and insight. I am watching over you to keep you safe from harm. You must continue on your journey, for you have a long way to go. Please, take this."

She held out a staff that had been carved out of wood, in the shape of a unicorn's horn. "Thank you," I said, as I placed my hand into the water to take it from her. As my hand made contact with the water, the ripples began to break up the image of the intriguing Priestess. I managed to get hold of the staff, then I heard her say, "Use it wisely. It is most powerful." And then she was gone.

THE FAIRY FOLK
Encountering the People of Cups

After continuing on my journey for some time, I stopped for a short break. Sitting down under a large tree, I heard strange noises coming from the forest. My curiosity got the better of me, so I decided to track down the noise, setting off the path and through the enchanted forest.

Set back a little way from the path, surrounded by trees, I beheld a beautiful fairy glade where several unicorns were gaily prancing. Each was only about the size of a small dog. I crept up slowly, trying not to frighten them away. I was convinced that they could not see me, and as I drew closer, I became aware that the unicorns weren't the only beings in this glade.

There were lots of little people too, men, women, and children, all dressed in medieval-type dress. I wanted to get a closer look, but as I put my foot forward I trod on a pile of twigs that cracked beneath my feet, shattering the peace. The little people heard me and scampered into the safety of the bushes. The unicorns also ran off.

"Please don't be frightened," I said, "I won't hurt you."

I looked around to see if anything was moving. Crouching down, I waited with bated breath. Gradually there were signs of life as a small unicorn came trotting from behind the trees. Fluttering around his head was a tiny unicorn, like the one that had fluttered about my head earlier. The unicorn showed no fear as he approached me and put his head on my lap. As I lifted my hand to stroke his white and silver mane, a little voice shouted out, "Don't hurt him!"

I looked up to see one of the little people running toward me. He was a mature, stocky little man. He wasn't much taller than the unicorn, and had long, flowing strawberry-blond hair and a bushy ginger beard. He was dressed in a long brown sack cloth with a brown cord tied around his middle, a bit like a monk. "Don't hurt him," he cried again. I reassured the little elf-like character that I had no intention of hurting anyone – and certainly not the unicorn.

How the Fairy Folk Came To Be

The man, whose name turned out to be Oz, asked me what I was doing in the glade. I began to explain about the Lady of the Star and the Silver Lake incident. I asked him if he knew the way to the enchanted castle.

"Which one?" he asked.

"What do you mean?"

Having warmed up to me, Oz sat down on a small log and began to tell me all about the enchanted lands and the fairy folk that lived here. "We are leprechauns. Our ancestors originated in Ireland many centuries ago. I belong to the suit of cups. We are known as the water people, and we came to these lands long ago when our own land became inhabited with too many humans." He explained that his ancestors had fled their country to find peace and tranquility among the unicorns.

The little leprechauns had been spiritually guided to this enchanted land. As time passed, they had different ideas as to who should lead the leprechauns. The four eldest of the tribe could not agree on certain points, so they decided to go their separate ways. The four groups of leprechauns formed four colonies, each with their own enchanted castle. Each colony has an affinity with a different element: water, fire, air, and earth. The different groups became known as the suit of cups, the suit of rods, the suit of swords, and the suit of pentacles. Each has their own royalty, comprising a king, queen, knight, and page. Sensing that I was curious to know more, Oz continued to explain more about the four suits.

Understanding the Four Suits

The Suit of Cups

The water people (suit of cups) are loving and very emotional. They make good parents and tend to concentrate their work on taking care of the very young, nursing the sick, and caring for the elderly.

The Suit of Swords

The air people (suit of swords) are very clever and quick-thinking. They are the inventors and teachers. They are also in charge of communications and all things concerning intelligence. It also snows a lot in their neck of the woods.

The Suit of Rods

The fire people (suit of rods) are the warriors and protect us all in times of need. They are full of fire and drive, and although a little stubborn in their attitude (convinced that they are superior), their intentions are well-meaning. It is decreed that they are the gatherers, providing all four leprechaun suits with food and other necessities.

The Suit of Pentacles

The earth people (suit of pentacles) are down-to-earth, logical people who take care of the finances and count the gold. They are very trustworthy, so it is decreed that they are the treasurers.

Although the leprechauns live in their own communities, they still help each other. For example, if a leprechaun belonging to the rods is wounded, it is a leprechaun from the suit of cups that comes to his aid and nurses him until he is better.

Understanding the Higher Law

I told Oz about my consultation with the Magician. "Which 'suit' does he belong to?" I asked. Oz explained that besides the four groups previously mentioned, in this enchanted world there is also a fifth group. This is the group of the higher law, the God-like royalty figures such as the Hierophant and the High Priestess that re-enforce the laws of life. The gods of birth and death are also among a higher breed of spiritual beings who are a force unto themselves.

"You will find them in the spiritual garden of peace that surrounds the palace on high." Oz said. "The Emperor and Empress live in the palace at the top of the spiritual, spiral path that ascends up to infinity, but one has to conquer the labyrinth of enchanted forest to reach this destination. You must have faith and trust to attain this goal."

I replied, quite truthfully, "Yes, I know."

By this time all the other fairy folk had come out from hiding behind the trees, to get a closer look at this "giant" talking to the old wise leprechaun. Although I must have seemed miles higher than them, they had realized by now that I posed no threat; they were not in any danger.

Oz clapped his hands, shouting, "A drink for the lady!" Two small, round leprechaun women scuffled out from the bushes. Gingerly, they approached me to inquire what I liked to eat. I informed them I was a vegetarian, to which they both sighed with great relief. Off they scurried, and when they reappeared a few minutes later they presented me with a drink in a tiny chalice, along with a small platter of food. I had worked up quite an appetite with the day's events, so it took quite a few chalices full of drink and platters full of food to satisfy me. Eventually I thanked them for their kind hospitality and bid them farewell as I continued my journey.

The Pentacle Fairy Folk

Oz had been kind enough to draw a map of the labyrinth for me, on which he indicated the way I should proceed. Once more I felt quite alone, until a familiar fluttering passed over my head – my little unicorn friend had joined me once again. I was pleased to see him. Together, we set off into the magical labyrinth.

A short while later, we stumbled across an elderly unicorn who was harnessed up to a rickety old cart. He looked weary as he slowly but surely pulled the cart full of pentacles along the path. The cart looked as though it weighed a ton; the poor unicorn was defiantly struggling to plod on. He seemed steadfast, as if nothing would deter him. It pained me to watch the unicorn struggle, so I went over to help him. I took hold of the cart on one side of the unicorn, trying to lift as well as pull. Now I was so close to the unicorn I could see marks on his back where the harness had rubbed him. We struggled along the road until we were greeted by the page of pentacles. He took the other side of the cart, which made the journey a lot easier. He chatted quite jovially about this and that, and we arrived at our destination in no time. We found ourselves in a quaint little village, full of thatched cottages. In the town center we saw a larger building with little leprechaun warriors standing outside the front entrance.

The page explained that this was our destination. The pentacles were to be unloaded here to enable the king of pentacles to count and store them all in a safe place. We were invited to tour this little township and meet the royals for high tea.

After some interesting talk and a delicious tea, the queen of pentacles (who was a kind, motherly figure) took me to one side and said softly, "Many things in life you can change, but many you cannot. We are the earth folk because we are down to earth, steadfast, and loyal. Be true to yourself, and you will attain your goal." I thanked her for her wisdom and bid farewell to the pentacle folk.

The sun was beginning to set, casting a warm reddish-orange glow upon the sky as if it were on fire. In the background I could see the enchanted palace on high, silhouetted in all its splendor. It was truly grand.

DISENCHANTED

I quickened my pace, for I wanted to cover as much ground as possible before nightfall. I had no method of illumination, even though my little unicorn friend glowed in the dusk. He was not quite bright enough to light the way in the dark. The bushes were so dense in places that I determined it would be far too dangerous for me to make my way in the dark. I figured I had about an hour before nightfall. So I began to run and was making good headway until my foot got caught up in something. I stumbled and fell to the ground. I lay there for a moment, and as I began to rise, my foot felt as though it was stuck fast. I pulled and pulled in an attempt to extricate myself, but it was to no avail. The little unicorn darted about trying to find a way to free me, but he was too tiny to do anything anyway.

Turning around to see what I was caught up on, I saw thick brown vines emerging out of the ground rapidly, twisting and entwining themselves around each other, wrapping themselves around my ankle. I looked up to see how far they reached, and to my amazement I saw two tall trees in the shape of two unicorns towering above me. Before I knew it, I was suspended between these two tall unicorn trees, just dangling in mid-air. How would I ever get out of this predicament?

Night began to fall and I was still hopelessly stuck. I tried shouting for help, hoping that Oz or one of his friends would come to my rescue, but the forest was still, not a sound to be heard at all. As I was suspended upside-down, the tiny unicorn settled on my foot and fell fast asleep.

I couldn't help wondering how long I would be left hanging there until someone found me. Then I realized that maybe there was a reason for this, a sort of moral – "less haste, less waste." I was so eager to cover as much ground as possible that maybe I was missing the whole point. Life is too short and precious to rush. Occasionally we have to stand still and take stock of our lives in order to become more in tune with ourselves. People have become so engrossed in the hustle and bustle of today's fast living that we tend to lose touch with our spirituality.

The Sword Fairy Folk

I must have fallen asleep because when I opened my eyes I was not suspended in the trees anymore. I was lying on a bed of golden brown leaves, and the little unicorn was curled up and asleep by my side. Dawn was breaking. As I looked out across the meadow, the orange-red glow from the rising sun gave the panoramic view a warm tinge. However, to my surprise, the ground was covered in a blanket of snow. I had the strangest feeling I had been here before. Time was pushing on, so I gently awakened the unicorn and we set off again. Although the snow lay quite thick on the ground, we were not cold. As I looked down, I noticed some little footprints in the snow. Just at that moment a small arrow flew past my face. It startled me, and I jumped back. The arrow stuck in one of the trees and it appeared to have something tied to it. My curiosity got the better of me so I went over to investigate. I could not see from whence it came, but sure enough, there was a note rolled up and attached to it. I unraveled the small scroll and read: "Welcome, Suzanne, we are expecting you." It went on to outline directions to the small township of the "air people," the suit of swords.

I was curious to meet these people and hoped we might be offered a little breakfast. I was not disappointed. Their township was not far from where we were, and as we approached we were greeted by a handsome young warrior on horseback. He took us to meet the king and queen of swords, who were most hospitable. They told us about the dangers to watch out for on the approach to the great palace on high. They described how they had lost one of their messengers to the demon king who lured the young warrior off the right path. When I asked what had become of this warrior, they both looked solemn. The king of swords said, "He paid for his mistake with his life."

I asked the king of swords if he sent more warriors out to seek revenge. The king replied that he had not, explaining, "Life and death are one, so in the beginning it shall be in the end, they are the Alpha and Omega. In the face of death we should look within, for deep within our hopes and aspirations we all have silent knowledge of beyond." I thought deeply about what he had said as I set off on my travels again.

The Rod Fairy Folk

The sun was high up in the sky now, and as the warm rays beat down on this enchanted land, the snow began to melt. Our next port of call was to be the settlement of the "fire people," the suit of rods. All the little houses there were crooked; even the little castle where the king and queen of rods lived bore twisted spires that looked like a horn from a unicorn.

Oz had told me that these people had inherited the true Irish blood. They all had either strawberry blond or flaming red hair and ruddy complexions. These were the warriors; most of the leprechaun men in this tribe worked with the unicorns, rounding them up and training them as work horses. All the unicorns were treated well, as they were seen as divine creatures. Anyone found guilty of inflicting pain or grief on such an animal was punished severely.

I spoke with a young leprechaun who had discovered through his studies in biology that the unicorn foal, when first born, had two horn buds, one on each side of his head. Instead of these buds developing into two horns, they grew toward each other, entwining as they grew, resulting in one long straight horn. This explains why the unicorn's horn is spiral shaped, while most horned animals have smooth horns.

As with human beings, the temperament of the unicorns varied, but on the whole they are gentle but strong. Most other animals have two horns, but the unicorn has only one; so it immediately has the advantage. Imagine a bull charging at a unicorn; the single horn is obviously a deadlier weapon.

The fire people were a fascinating source of information about unicorns, but I could see the enchanted palace clearly now and felt it was time to push on. A great sense of excitement filled me as I could see that my little unicorn guide and I were soon to reach our destination.

THE GARDEN OF SPIRITUAL LOVE

The forest did not appear to be so dense now. In fact, it began to open up into a beautiful, peaceful plain. I saw signs of life as I approached the clearing. Two young lovers lounged in the grass. Just then a unicorn flew past me. He had beautiful white wings that spanned out about six feet, and he looked quite elegant in flight. To my left, sitting on a tree stump, a young man was serenading a young woman with his mandolin. Everything was so peaceful; I felt as though I could stay there forever. However, I was curious to find out what was waiting for me at the Enchanted Palace. As we continued along, a girl, who had just been playing and prancing with a unicorn foal, ran up to us. She held a garland of red and white roses in her hand.

"These are for you," she said, and I bent down while she placed them around my neck. "Thank you," I replied. This must be the Garden of Spiritual Love, I realized; red roses represent true love, and white roses signify pure spiritual love. Feeling serene, I continued on.

TESTING TIME

Eventually we came to the spiritual path that led to the Palace. At the foot of the pathway was a stone building in the shape of a unicorn. It gave the impression that it had been a grand building in its day, but I could not help thinking that something was wrong. Upon closer inspection I realized that this unicorn statue was crumbling. Large boulders and pieces of rubble began to break loose, falling from the statue's head and tumbling down toward the ground. As I looked up again, I realized a large boulder was heading straight for me. I panicked – I knew I could not run fast enough to escape, and I really believed my time had come. Suddenly, I felt something grab me around the waist and whisk me away from danger. I heard the boulder crash to the ground behind me.

I found myself ascending into the air on the back of a large, muscular stallion unicorn, and my little friend was fluttering desperately to keep up. I put my hand out and managed to catch him without crushing him. I put him safely into my pocket. In front of me sat a bare-backed warrior with long auburn hair. Although we could not have been in the air more than a few minutes, it all seemed to fly past like a slow-motion dream. The feeling of flying through the air was incredible. I had felt nothing like it before in my whole life – it was truly exhilarating. The warrior flew us toward the spiritual path, and although he never spoke a word to me, I knew he represented strength. In no time at all we landed, and the warrior helped me down from the unicorn. He bid me farewell without even a word passing his lips, just a warm smile before he galloped off into the distance.

The little unicorn and I started to make our way up the path. It was very steep but we persevered – we must have gone about two hundred yards when we were faced with a choice. The path split into two directions. So determined was I to reach the end of my quest, I completely forgot about keeping to the right hand path. I just took off without thinking. However, it was not long before I realized what I had done: I had taken the other path.

My concentration on reaching the top was broken by the sound of crying. I glanced up and saw a young girl sobbing, head in hands. She was curled up on a rock in the fetal position. By her side was a small unicorn who looked very unhappy, as though he was grieving for his mistress.

I was going to ask her what was the matter, but at that moment the unicorn looked straight at me and an overwhelming feeling of sorrow came upon me. Without speaking a word, the unicorn communicated with me: something awful had befallen the young girl. She had been lured into a false sense of security and then had paid the price for her folly. She felt imprisoned within her own emotions, desperately unhappy, punishing herself mentally for letting herself become involved with the evil temptations that had been sent to test her. The poor little unicorn by her side had tried to warn her of the perils, but to no avail, for she would not listen to reason. Now she suffers because she has become her own worst enemy, but the unicorn foal is truly faithful and remains by her side forever more.

The demon king (Devil) had corrupted her virtue. I felt his presence – he must have been still lurking around somewhere in the vicinity. Just at that very moment a terrible blood-curdling scream filled the air, and the Devil appeared. He leaped down from what appeared to be a great height, but as I turned to see where he had come from there was nothing.

Startled, I tried my utmost not to show my fear. As he came closer I could see he was half human and half beast. He crouched on a rock like a wild cat ready to pounce on his prey. He had two horns protruding from his forehead, surrounded by long swirling hair, blacker than the darkest night. His face, I thought, was quite handsome, but his deep green eyes were cold and callous. He had long narrow pupils, like those of a cat.

"Well, Neophyte, not so innocent now, are we!" he said.

"What do you mean?" I replied.

"When you began your search you knew nothing of this Enchanted Land, yet now you believe you are invincible. Why seek you the unattainable?" he said with a smirk on his face. He looked as if he may have been quite a good-looking man once upon a time, but his expressions and mannerisms made him ugly.

"I admit I don't know everything, but I have learned a lot from my experiences on this journey," I exclaimed. At that the demon frowned and said, "Let's see just how much you've learned! If you can outsmart the forces of evil then I shall let you go back to the right hand path."

"And if I cannot?"

"Then you are mine for eternity," he said, and vanished.

I was really scared but I was determined not to let it show. I turned to head back to the right path, but as I began to run the ground started to crumble underneath my feet. The path suddenly began shaking and I felt myself getting hotter and hotter. At that point the earth cracked open completely, and billowing smoke and flames engulfed me. I began choking on the smoke.

As I looked down I saw that the ground had opened up completely. I was right on the edge – a little further and I would surely fall down into the underworld.

Then a voice spoke; it sounded like a voice from the past. My grandmother appeared as an apparition in the swirling smoke. "Suzanne! Use the staff," she said. The staff? For a moment I did not know what she meant; then I remembered the staff, given to me by the lady in the lake. I fumbled in my pocket and pulled out the staff. To this day I don't know what came over me, but in spite of the smoke stifling me, I managed to shout out, "No! I will not submit, in the name of the unicorn! In love and peace I trust! I will not give in!"

The staff began to glow in my hand. It was a pulsating light that sparked off in every direction like fireworks. The sparks of good fought with the fires of Hell until it ended with a mighty explosion. The ground stopped shaking and the smoke cleared. The choking sensation vanished from my throat. I stood up, but then I saw the demon before me.

"Evil is in the power of the mind, and I don't believe in you!" I said.

"You fool!" he cried, "Now you must die!"

"No," I said. "It is you who must die." I threw the unicorn staff with all my might. It flew through the air like an arrow and speared the demon right through his upper torso.

As he fell to the ground, a terrible piercing shriek filled the air, chilling me to the bone. I watched in amazement as he beckoned to me and began to shrivel up until he was nothing more than a slimy green puddle on the floor. He had completely disappeared. A great sense of relief filled me. I had won.

Now I faced another problem: How was I to get across the gaping hole in the pathway? I reached into my top pocket to see if my little friend was still there, and to make sure he was all right. He was a little shaken, but he seemed fine. I asked him if he would fly off to summon help, so that we might cross this large crevice. He immediately flew away as though he had understood every word I had spoken.

Within a few minutes, I heard a noise like the sound of rumbling wheels rolling at great speed and coming toward me. I turned and saw my little friend leading two magnificent unicorns pulling a golden chariot. At the helm was a woman warrior. In her right hand was a royal blue flag that sported a unicorn motif. She pulled on the reins tightly and both unicorns and chariot came quickly to a halt. This woman had an air of authority. She looked straight at me and spoke.

"You have conquered the powers of evil and rid the land of this horrible beast." She beckoned me into her chariot, then at great speed, we took off and flew over the crevice to the right path. The warrior congratulated me for being so brave and courageous. I climbed down and waved goodbye as she sped off.

I began a steep ascent, careful to look down to avoid falling off the path, which appeared to be suspended in mid-air. I looked behind me to see how far I had come. To my astonishment, a gaunt figure stood behind me in a long dark robe. He was holding a scythe in his hand and reminded me somewhat of the Grim Reaper of death. Behind him stood the remains of a unicorn – beyond that there was nothing. The path I had traveled had disappeared. I had no wish to brush shoulders with death, so I continued up the path. The king of swords had told me, "In the depths of your desire for life lies your silent knowledge of the beyond." With this in mind, I was no longer scared.

THE ENCHANTED PALACE ON HIGH

We eventually reached our destination, entering the palace through pearl-encrusted gates. The vision we beheld was amazing. In the center of the massive marble entrance room was a tall crystal fountain. On the top of the fountain, two carved crystal cherubs poured water into a large bowl; while lower down in the bowl, crystal unicorns dipped their horns into the water. The floor was made of marble, and the walls were crystal with horn-shaped arches for doorways.

Trumpets blew a fanfare for the grand entrance of the Emperor and Empress. Two little leprechauns rushed in with a chair apiece for the monarchs to be seated. They knew everything about me, and told me that they had been expecting my arrival. I asked them how they knew about me, why they were expecting me; to which they replied that all budding clairvoyants must be tested for their gifted abilities.

The path I had traveled was similar to the story of the tarot: one is born naive, knowing nothing (the Fool), and must travel through the experiences of life (the Major Arcana). Unfortunately, some do not come though the trial period as well as I had. But I had not succumbed to greed or been power-hungry, and I had conquered the forces of evil.

I was told that the Hierophant wished to see me. I felt highly honored. The Emperor and Empress led me into another room, this one even more elegant than the first. In this room stood a grand altar, behind which raised up a large golden throne.

An old man with white hair and a long white beard was seated upon this throne. He wore a golden crown filled with sapphires. A brilliant white light surrounded him, filling the whole room. This god-like figure was the Hierophant. I immediately fell to my knees, bowing in respect to this almighty figure of authority, wisdom, and spiritual love. He told me to rise, but my knees were trembling, my legs felt like jelly; so much so that I was surprised I was able to stand. I gazed in amazement at the Hierophant. He smiled back at me and said, "I bless you." Just at that moment, the brilliant white light around him seemed to be getting brighter and brighter, until it was dazzling me. I was unable to see anything else for the light.

The most beautiful feeling I had ever felt engulfed me. I was at peace within myself, feeling contented and happy. I felt no pain. All the aches I had from walking for so long had vanished completely. Still dazzled by the brightness, I was drawn to the light. I heard a voice whispering my name over and over again.

It felt as if I were floating through a long tunnel of white and gold light. I recognized the voice as it became louder. I had a lump in my throat, and my eyes welled up with tears.

"Nanna!" I cried.

I saw her face emerging through the brilliant white light at the end of the tunnel. She appeared radiant, with beautiful jet black hair, and those warm brown eyes so deep they could melt ice. Her skin was whiter than white, and her lips were wearing the same old reassuring smile that I remembered so well. Her dainty hand reached out toward me through the bright light. As I held my hand out, her hand touched mine. I remember thinking how cold she felt. I just wanted to embrace her, but she said she could not come any closer, as it was time for me to go back.

She said she would be waiting for me on the other side. I was not to be scared, for passing over was painless. She told me she was at peace now, and how she loved the beautiful roses in the gardens. As she handed me a white rose, our fingers touched again for the last time. I could feel her slipping away from me. Her final words to me were, "Remember me, for if my voice should fade in your ears, my love shall live in your heart."

Almost choking on the lump in my throat, my eyes filled with tears; I understood Nanna had to go, but I had missed her for so long. I could not help myself from crying out, "Please don't go! Please don't go."

.◆. .◆. .◆.

I don't remember much after that. I do recall finding myself under the green shady tree in Sapphire Valley. I must have fallen fast asleep after my picnic.

To this day I am not sure if those events really occurred, or if I dreamed them. They certainly felt real. In fact, later that same night, I discovered a white rose and a tiny horse-shoe in my pocket.

Chapter 2

The Tarot

There are many myths and legends connected with the origins of the tarot. It is believed that tarot cards were actually invented for play, and are the predecessor of the normal deck of playing cards we see today. Centuries ago, the Romany gypsy people spread the word about the ability to foresee the future through the use of tarot. (The reason tarot cards are pictorial instead of written is because many people were unable to read in those days.) Tarot portrays one's journey through life, representing the experiences that we all have to go through (at one time or another) as part of growing up.

As a tarot reader, you must take great care in counseling your clients. Some people are simply curious, and will take from your reading what they want to take in. Others will turn to you quite seriously for advice and guidance through consulting the tarot. Some people are of a nervous disposition and may tend to hang on your every word. People also tend to fear the unknown. Therefore it is of the utmost importance that you choose your words carefully so as not to scare anyone!

Many people have asked me over the years if the tarot is "evil." There is nothing evil about a deck of tarot cards; the only danger is the possibility of misinterpretation. This is why it is most important that you interpret the card reading as accurately as possible. Don't just read the isolated meaning of a card. Taking into account the cards in the surrounding spread will give you a clearer picture. If any doubt lingers about the reading, ask your client to take another card until the whole picture starts to make sense.

For instance, if the card you are reading is a negative one, but it is surrounded by bright, optimistic cards, then the outcome will be positive. You will find as time goes on that your tarot cards actually talk to you and give you a great deal of insight into all sorts of situations.

Remember that the tarot is here to guide you. Through reading tarot cards, you can learn about certain situations forthcoming that you may not have been expecting. It is most encouraging to know about opportunities coming up in your future, and to be guided in the right direction. This enables you to take the best course of action when the time is right. People are often desperate to know when a negative situation will end. You must always give hope and encouragement, for we are all masters of our own destiny. The predictions of the tarot are only indications of what could happen if alternative or remedial action is not taken.

TAROT FOR BEGINNERS
Familiarizing Yourself With the Unicorn Tarot

Some say that it is bad luck to buy your own tarot cards, and that it is better to let someone else buy them for you. However, there is nothing worse than being all excited about opening your first tarot deck only to realize that you can't use it because the pictures mean nothing to you. Therefore it makes sense to browse through the many different tarot decks available today until you find the one that you feel comfortable with.

The Unicorn Tarot is easy to use, and I recommend it for beginning and professional tarot readers alike. I suggest that you first familiarize yourself with these cards before trying to rush straight into doing readings. Place your cards under your pillow and sleep on them for the first few weeks. You should play with your new tarot deck a little each day, being careful not to overdo it the first time they're out of the packet.

Preparation for
Reading the Cards

Before reading the cards it is always advisable to clear your mind of all distractions and other thoughts. You may find "deep breathing" exercises will help to relax you, dispelling all of the day's frustrations, bringing you in line and consequently at peace with yourself.

It is spiritually enlightening to meditate on a tarot card before you go to bed. Just take one card from the Major Arcana per night and study it carefully before putting it back in the pack and placing it under your pillow. Then "sleep on it." Try meditating on a different card every night until you have completed the full set of Major Arcana cards. This will bring you more spiritually in tune with the unicorn and will help to open your psychic channels or "third eye."

The Unicorn Tarot Deck

The Unicorn Tarot deck consists of 78 cards. These are divided into two sets: 22 Major Arcana and 56 Minor Arcana, the latter being similar to regular playing card decks.

The Major Arcana

The Major Arcana of the Unicorn Tarot is as follows:

     0 The Fool
     I The Magician
     II The High Priestess
     III The Empress
     IV The Emperor
     V The Hierophant
     VI The Lovers
     VII The Chariot
     VIII Strength
     IX The Hermit
     X Wheel of Fortune
     XI Justice
     XII The Hanged Man
     XIII Death
     XIV Temperance
     XV The Devil
     XVI The Tower
     XVII The Star
     XVIII The Moon
     XIX The Sun
     XX Judgment
     XXI The World

The Minor Arcana

The Minor Arcana is divided into four suits (as with playing cards): cups (hearts), pentacles (diamonds), rods (clubs), and swords (spades). Each of the four suits consists of cards numbered ace through ten. There are four court cards in each suit: page, knight, queen, and king.

Chapter 3

The Major Arcana

0 The Fool

The Fool can be seen as the "Babe of the Abyss," representing the beginning of the spiritual journey through life: as is the beginning, so is the end. As everything runs through the cycle, from birth we have a childlike innocence, a willingness to learn, and an eagerness to try out new experiences.

Here the Fool is naive, ready to take chances and not stopping to think of the consequences before he rushes on ahead. He is prancing with his head in the clouds; he doesn't see that he is dancing on edge of the cliff. One wonders if he will fall, or will he be lucky enough to turn just in time? He seems to live for the moment.

The unicorn is more spiritual and wise. He can see what dangers may lie ahead. He rears to try to catch the Fool's attention, but will the Fool listen to the warning? Or will he rush headlong into what could only end up being great trouble and strife for him? Remember the saying, "Fools rush in where angels fear to tread."

DIVINATORY MEANING: When the Fool appears in the spread, it is likely that you are quite enthusiastic about a situation. However, you may be in danger of jumping in feet first,

0 THE FOOL

only thinking about the consequences afterwards when it's too late! Take into consideration the cards around the Fool, and the context of your question. For instance, if you're asking about relationships, then you must keep your feet firmly on the ground. There is a strong tendency for you to let your emotions rule your head.

On the other hand, if the question is in connection with career or money, you should execute extreme caution (although you may be very excited about a new money-making opportunity), or else you could lose out financially.

REVERSED MEANING: The Fool is not only excitable but is likely to be very foolish about the situation pertaining to the question at hand. You could say or do something in the heat of the moment that will most certainly be regretted later. This could be a result of being over-optimistic about the situation. You must take extreme caution, and avoid taking risks of all kinds, as you cannot trust your own feelings right now and could be making a big mistake.

I The Magician

The Magician is depicted juggling his tools. Each tool represents one of the four elements: cups symbolize water and emotions; pentacles signify the earth, practicality, and earthly wealth such as gold; swords represent the air element, representing intelligence and strength; and to complete the full set, the Magician holds his powerful unicorn horn rod (representing fire) in his left hand. This serves as his magic wand. The Magician looks as though he is about to conjure something up.

The unicorn on the right side of the Magician is a more mature, wise stallion. He appears to be watching the Magician's every move, for although this is a very clever and quick-thinking man, one can never be too sure what trick he may have hidden up his long, flowing sleeves.

This man is a law unto himself; he is powerful and clever, but sometimes too cunning for his own good. The questioner must guard against being tricked or manipulated by this man. The unicorn is inspired by this Magician, but even this spiritually intelligent beast is wary of his powers. The Magician needs the unicorn's magical horn to make his spells work, and the unicorn needs the Magus in order to stay alive. Man almost made the unicorn extinct once before.

DIVINATORY MEANING: When the Magician appears in the cards, positive cards surrounding him could be a sign that a positive, quick-thinking man is entering your life. He will bring out the best in you, spiritually inspiring you to be more creative in thoughts and efforts. Even if you come up against obstacles, these problems will be resolved as if by magic.

I THE MAGICIAN

REVERSED MEANING: Caution is needed now, for in real life the Magus could show himself to be a confidence trickster, causing you upset and problems. Be warned: he is a quick-thinking and quick-talking person who never misses a trick and is very credible. He can charm the birds out of the trees (if it suits him to do so), but if he doesn't get his own way, he will throw tantrums and cause a great deal of upset. You can't reason with him when he is in this frame of mind. In his eyes, he is the one who is never wrong. Do not make any agreements with this man as he is not a man of his word.

II *The High Priestess*

The High Priestess is portrayed here as pure and virtuous with her long, flowing virginal gown. She stands with her magic glowing rod in her left hand.

Gently trotting beside her, the unicorn (who is attracted by her beauty) protects the High Priestess from any danger with his spiritual strength. This feminine Goddess figure possesses great psychic powers and depth of insight, and she has the ability to perform miracles. She may appear cool and aloof with hidden depths of wisdom, but she is a strong, self-sufficient, secretive beauty with hidden powers. She knows you better than you know yourself. She appears in real life as a business woman, maybe a counselor or psychic advisor. She is a listener with the spiritual gift to be able to advise you with your problems.

DIVINATORY MEANING: The High Priestess represents a strong-minded, self-sufficient, mature woman (if not mature in years then mature in mind). Like the true Goddess that she is, she is full of sexual personal magnetism, yet she remains untouchable to most. It would be beneficial for you to trust in this woman and listen to what she may have to say, as she can advise you with her strong intuitive powers of persuasion.

This card can also represent achievement and attainment of goals. It will sometimes come up in the card spreads of those successfully taking exams, where the outcome is most certainly glorious achievement. The High Priestess could also be advising you to draw upon your own spiritual

II THE HIGH PRIESTESS

intuition. This is a very feminine card and can indicate fertility, especially if it is surrounded by the Empress, the Lovers, or the ace of cups.

REVERSED MEANING: This can indicate that a woman is not using her gifts to the best advantage. She may appear to be quite shallow, even unapproachable. In some instances, depending on the surrounding cards (whether they are positive or negative), the High Priestess may be using her powers of persuasion to manipulate people into doing what she wants them to do. Sooner or later she will be found out, and no good will come from it.

III THE EMPRESS

III The Empress

The Empress symbolizes Mother Nature, the fruitful Goddess of fertility. She has a voluptuous figure and the glow of motherhood. At her feet is a baby unicorn who is obviously quite content. She is the earth mother, a loving woman who represents your relationship with your mother, wife, or any woman who influences your life and offers advice, guidance, and protection. The Empress is the symbol of growth, fruitful outcome, and the harvest time when we reap what we have sown. She brings with her fresh life and new beginnings.

DIVINATORY MEANING: When the Empress appears in the card spread it suggests fertility and growth. If the cards surrounding are cups (particularly the ace of cups or the three of cups), then the fruitful outcome is of an emotional nature, such as a birth or addition to the family. If the surrounding cards are pentacles, the outcome will be connected with work or finances. There may be a windfall of money or a promotion at work. If rods surround, creativity shall be heightened. If swords surround, your agile mind will bring victory over upset.

REVERSED MEANING: When the Empress appears reversed in the spread, you have to determine the association. If you are a woman who wants to know about health, this card placed reversed can indicate miscarriage or infertility. If you are asking about work, or the surrounding cards are pentacles, it could be an indication that you are over-indulgent and may spend far too much money, or you are being wasteful. If you are a man, this placing indicates that there is a possessive or protective feminine force in your life who could stifle your progress.

IV The Emperor

The Emperor symbolizes an authoritative figure, a counselor, or a father figure. He is a strong-minded man who has worked hard to get to where he is and demands respect. Sometimes you may feel that he is unapproachable; but you must remember he is only human. In his right hand he holds the magical unicorn horn. At his feet is a young unicorn foal, showing the Emperor's role as the great protector and master of all he serves. He is ready to advise you as a father figure, for he is a fair arbitrator of law and order. Although you would associate the Emperor with being married to the Empress, there is an air of aloofness around him. In real life he could be the sort of person who becomes quite wrapped up in his work or career. He appears to be living in his own little world, leaving relationships in the background.

DIVINATORY MEANING: You may be faced with having to deal with an authoritative figure. If surrounding cards are Justice or Judgment, then the immediate situation could be one of a legal nature, in which the Emperor may be of help in giving sound advice on how to handle the situation. Although you may feel anxious, you must not overreact to established rules and regulations,.

REVERSED MEANING: This could represent a tendency to become too domineering, even tyrannical, about your life. You have an inclination to become power-hungry (misusing authority) to the extent of hurting others. This will only serve to cause trouble when someone tells you frankly what they think of you.

IV THE EMPEROR

V THE HIEROPHANT

V The Hierophant

The Hierophant is the wise spiritual ruler. He has great powers of perception; what he says, goes, for although he doesn't speak very often, everyone sits up and takes notice when he does. The young unicorn in this picture is about to rise to his feet and do as his Master commands. This man is steadfast in his beliefs. He sticks rigidly to the old traditions and spiritual beliefs and is not open to persuasion.

When you ask for guidance, and this card appears, it is most often saying "leave it to God." You may feel stuck in a rut, but there is not a lot you can do about it right now. Return your thoughts to previous times in your life when you were faced with similar situations. Learn by your experiences; the path of life is a spiritual journey and we learn as we go along.

DIVINATORY MEANING: It may now be time to widen your breadth of vision. You may be approaching a time of change, whether you want it or not. You need guidance, so take the advice of others; although ultimately it is your decision as to which path to take. Sometimes it helps to see another person's point of view and learn by their mistakes.

REVERSED MEANING: You feel discontented with the way things are in your life at this time, and feel that there must be more to life than this. It is time to break out of your rut and find something new to inspire you. Meeting new people is good spiritual stimulation and will help you to find yourself; it is as though you are on a soul search now. Maybe you need something new to believe in or a soulmate to inspire new beginnings.

VI The Lovers

Two Lovers caress each other, succumbing to their strong urges to be as one. Above them hovers a winged unicorn, whose magical powers (unbeknownst to the loving couple) have brought them together. However, lurking on a branch in the tree is a serpent, an untrustworthy evil tempter who likes to indulge in wrongdoings and causes disaster wherever it goes!

All relationships go through a testing period at some time. Depending on the people involved and how the situation is handled, this "test" will determine the fate of the Lovers.

The unicorn, representing true spirituality, is protecting the Lovers in this card. Against this serpent's wishes, their love is a spiritual one, soulmates as well as physical Lovers. They don't just want pleasures of the flesh; it is a love and intimacy comprising mind, body, and spirit, an intense karmic love. It is their destiny.

DIVINATORY MEANING: You are full of personal magnetism, with a strong possibility of a relationship developing. This will be more than just a physical attraction; the potential is for a uniting of soulmates or even reincarnated lovers from a past life. If this card appears in the spread with the ace of cups or the four of rods, it means marriage and bonding. If the Star is close by, then it is truly a dream come true. However, if negative cards are surrounding the Lovers, you must proceed with caution, as there may be some opposition to this relationship.

REVERSED MEANING: The Lovers reversed could indicate separation or even divorce, particularly if the Devil or the

VI THE LOVERS

ace of swords is close by. A destructive relationship is indicated, maybe due to jealousy or possessiveness. The unicorn loses his power of protection when reversed, and rather than a spiritual bond between the Lovers, the serpent indicates that this is more of a lustful, sexual attraction, and therefore is doomed to fail.

VII *The Chariot*

Apart from the obvious meaning of travel, the Chariot card represents change, challenge, and your strength and ability to overcome obstacles. See in the picture how the warrior has tight hold of the reins: she is in control. However, the brace of unicorns appear to be pulling in opposite directions, representing one's mind pulling one way while emotions are pulling the other way. Logic and emotions both need to be harnessed together in order for peace and tranquility to reign.

The woman warrior is holding her flag erect as if to imply victory. She is determined to forge ahead with whatever it takes to be triumphant. She represents a self-sufficient "go-getter" who is highly motivated and doesn't need anyone to help her achieve her goals.

DIVINATORY MEANING: When the Chariot appears in the spread, you must go full steam ahead into the project that you are contemplating now. You have the strength and ability to succeed even though the path ahead may seem a little bumpy at times. Triumph will reign in the end, but goals must be realized first without wasting valuable energy by pulling in several directions at once. All energies must be directed toward attaining the goal.

VII THE CHARIOT

This card also suggests a decision may need to be made, one that will alter the course of your life. When the World and/or the ace of pentacles are near, it can mean social or business travel.

REVERSED MEANING: This placing warns you not to spread energies too far and wide, or you will suffer the consequences. You may have little regard for rules and regulations, or the law of the land. Through a "power-hungry" quest for achievement, you may appear ruthless, bringing upon your own failure.

If the surrounding cards indicate travel, then this means breakdown, or trouble with a vehicle causing delayed journeys.

VIII Strength

The Strength card portrays a strong warrior sitting astride a beautiful but highly spirited unicorn mare. The mare is rearing up and ready for action, and yet there is still a feeling of eloquence. The unicorn knows her inner strength, and therefore has no need to prove herself. Although the unicorn is one of the most placid spiritual beasts, there is no doubt that her advantage above all other beasts is her long, powerful horn in the center of her forehead. Any two-horned animal would be no match for this supernatural beast.

The unicorn has the ability to bring peace out of conflict, and the warrior is a tower of strength who has no wish to harm anyone. It is in his nature to be a great protector.

DIVINATORY MEANING: When the Spiritual Warrior is with you in the form of the Strength card, you have the spiritual protection of the unicorn and are full of personal mag-

VIII STRENGTH

netism. You're energetic and healthy enough to forge ahead and achieve victory. This card also represents the strong, silent type of person, who is steadfast and loyal. If this pertains to a person coming into your life, you may rest assured that this person is a tower of strength and a good influence.

REVERSED MEANING: A weakening of strength is indicated here. Whether it is mentally, through stress; or physically, bringing a warning of ill health, depending on the surrounding cards. Negative energies could turn to aggression. You need to think more positively about your situation.

If this card appears when you are asking about finances or relationships, there will be a feeling of insecurity in these areas.

IX The Hermit

This card portrays the Hermit as a wise old man, resembling a monk. He is standing on the top of the highest spiritual path, and around his magical staff the winds of time swirl like mist. He holds the lamp of spiritual enlightenment to guide his way.

By his side stands an equally wise, unfettered unicorn. He is the spiritual companion to the Hermit, bringing with him his own inner reflection. The wondrous beast does not need to speak, for the Hermit is omniscient.

The Hermit may be interpreted as a withdrawal into one's self, but sometimes in life we all need a little time to ourselves in order to reflect on the life lessons we have experienced so that we may prepare ourselves for the future. Therefore, the Hermit also refers to knowledge, learning, and teaching; he is the sage or mentor of life's path and beyond.

IX THE HERMIT

DIVINATORY MEANING: When the spiritually unfettered unicorn comes to you via the Hermit card, it is an indication of a time of reflection. This may come as a period of
study and learning in order to better yourself or improve
your quality of life. You should meditate, or perhaps enroll in
an educational course, or seek advice and direction from a
learned source. Maybe it is time to sit down with a good book
so that you may become enlightened by inspirational litera-
ture. A period of solitude is now upon you, so use it wisely as
life is too short to waste time.

REVERSED MEANING: When the Hermit appears
reversed, you may be feeling very alone, as though no one
understands you. A feeling of "you vs. the world" is upon you
at the moment. It is a very lonely time, but may not be without reason. You practically become the Hermit, withdrawing
into yourself, blocking out family and friends. The surrounding cards will indicate the reason why you have become isolated. If Death is surrounding this card, you may have suffered the loss of a loved one and are consumed with grief.

X The Wheel of Fortune

The Wheel of Fortune depicts a dark, mysterious woman
crouched down with a large wheel in her hands. She looks as
though she is about to spin it on the ground like a coin, to
gamble as to whether it will come up heads or tails.

At many points in our lives, we are given an opportunity to
take a chance. The Wheel of Fortune is always turning in
someone's life, bringing unexpected changes or opportunities.
Behind the woman we can see the golden spires of a castle,

X THE WHEEL OF FORTUNE

indicating the good fortune and prosperity that the Wheel of Fortune may bring. The spiritual unicorn sits in excited anticipation by the wheel. This magical beast seems to have a smile on his face as if he already knows the outcome. The blood red rose in the foreground is a picture of beauty; however, if you are tempted to pick it, be warned: the poisonous thorns on the stem will harm you.

People that gamble may make a fortune, but may also lose a lot. The luck element depends on the surrounding cards and the way in which the card is placed, i.e., upright or reversed. **DIVINATORY MEANING:** There is no such thing as coincidence in the eyes of the unicorn; everything that happens in life happens for a reason. However, sometimes we are not aware of what is in store for us. You should expect the unexpected, as you are in for a pleasant surprise in the near future as long as you remain flexible. Expect a sudden change; the area of your life in which this change will take place is determined by the placement of this card in the spread or by the surrounding cards. If the ace of pentacles is nearby, you are likely to come into some money (a fortune). If the Lovers are nearby, a new love affair or sudden change for the better in your lovelife can be expected. Good luck and changes for the better are predominant.

REVERSED MEANING: Bad timing can lead to disastrous consequences now. Take heed! A fortune may be lost. Bad luck is on the horizon, causing frustrations, setbacks, delays, misunderstandings, hidden expenses, or unexpected bills. Tread very cautiously now, and seek spiritual advice before being pricked by the thorns of the rose again. Life changes are called for.

XI Justice

The Justice card depicts balance and harmony as a strong-minded goddess figure standing in between two beautiful unicorn pillars. This is a picture of power, strength, and unity.

In one hand the goddess holds the scales of Justice, law, and order. In the other hand she holds the spiritual sword of strength and fairness, indicating that all situations need to be carefully considered. Justice will prevail; the right solution will be found.

The sword and scales portrayed here indicate physical Justice, while the pair of unicorn pillars stands for spiritual or even karmic Justice. They remind us to do unto others as we would have them do unto us.

The Holy Spirits work in mysterious ways, yet ours is not to question why. The authoritative female figure may take strong measures to ensure that Justice will be done. You will get what you deserve (one way or the other) depending on which way the card falls and what cards surround it.

DIVINATORY MEANING: When Justice appears in the spread, you would be well advised to first consider whether you are making judgment on a situation in your life, or if a judgment is being made on you. This could pertain to dealings with authority figures, members of council, or pending legal matters. The good news is, if such matters do pertain to you, then you can be assured that the outcome will be successful and fair. Adopt a fair and merciful attitude to the situation at hand, avoiding the temptation to be one-sided or conceited about what you perceive to be fair. It is important to maintain a clear perspective.

XI JUSTICE

REVERSED MEANING: Injustice or prejudice is a possibility with this placing. You must consider the other cards carefully, as an illegal act may be taking place, especially if the Devil card is positioned close by.

There could be a karmic lesson to learn now. Proceed with extreme caution, or the result may be your own undoing. On the other hand, the injustice may be what you are suffering due to the actions of another. Fair play is called for at this time. Seek legal guidance if necessary.

XII The Hanged Man

The Hanged Man is the Fool who began his journey through life as the Babe of the Abyss, and is now at the stage where he has to make a big decision. He must look deep within himself, drawing upon the experiences that he has already gone through in his life in order to make the right decision. Before he can proceed, he must experience self-sacrifice. For now the stone effigies of the spiritual unicorn have risen up from the ground, holding the Hanged Man fast to make him stop and think.

"I am at a crossroads in my life now!" he says. "I cannot go back, I can only go forward!"

He is right, but he needs to think carefully because he is in a standstill period, whether he wants it or not. He must learn to endure the frustrations of not being in control for a while. Hands tied behind his back, the Hanged Man is unable to do anything about his present situation until the spiritual unicorn decides when the time is right. He must be prepared to give something up, to sacrifice something, and be able to learn from his experiences.

DIVINATORY MEANING: When the Hanged Man appears in the spread, you have no control over your present situation and must learn to bide time. You must also prepare for change, as you are at a turning point in which the old is forgotten and you start anew. You must learn to let go of an idea, hope, or situation pertaining to the past.

The surrounding cards will help to determine the reason why this situation has come to pass. If surrounded by cups, it may be as a result of frustrations in relationships. On the

XII THE HANGED MAN

other hand, it could be loss of job and enforced rest, if pentacles are close by. If the Hanged Man is surrounded by Death, the ace of swords, or the Tower, beware of suicidal tendencies due to a feeling of not being able to cope anymore. Try to maintain hope and a belief in your strength to overcome such problems.

REVERSED MEANING: When the Hanged Man appears reversed in a spread, you are ready to take the unicorn by the horn. Having come through your "lost soul" period, due to circumstances beyond your control, you are now ready to take some positive action.

XIII Death

Death is depicted by the Grim Reaper, standing in barren, desolate lands. No sun shines, nor birds sing; the dried ground is parched and cracked. All that remains is the skeleton of the unicorn, faithful and true even beyond Death.

It is said that the only way to kill a unicorn is to chop off his magical horn, for without it he has no strength nor the will to survive. Therefore, the picture denotes the beginning of the spiritual re-creation of the unicorn. This card is not always as black as it's painted, for although it does sometimes signify physical death, it also represents rebirth, fresh starts, and new beginnings. True, the Reaper does hold his sickle in his hands – but as the Fool learns on his journey, life is a cycle of birth, growth, knowledge through experience, and finally death, only to begin again. It is a never-ending cycle: the Alpha and the Omega. The spirit of the unicorn always gives us hope.

XIII DEATH

DIVINATORY MEANING: When Death appears in your spread, it signifies the end to an important situation or phase in your life. Examine the surrounding cards to assess the area of your life to which this pertains. In my experience reading tarot, I have found that people become quite distressed when this card appears. Thus it is most important that you remember that Death can be the end of a phase in life and the start of a fresh one; not necessarily the death of a person. You are about to emerge into something positive in your life, as when the caterpillar transforms into a chrysalis and finally into a butterfly.

REVERSED MEANING: You are in a situation that is gradually decaying. You must try to seriously consider what it is in your life that is not doing any good anymore. It could be a relationship growing stale, or a negative work environment needing to be changed. You may be bottling a lot of grief and upset within yourself. Let go. Clear away the dead wood in your life in order to make way for progress.

XIV Temperance

High in the spiritual retreat of the mountains, the Angel of Temperance stands, carefully pouring the waters of life from one chalice into another. She can not afford to spill any, as the waters of life represent the emotions and life force of mortals, so she takes great care.

A unicorn foal lays in front of her, patiently emulating the angelic qualities of hidden energy and spiritual strength. This implies that the Fool on his spiritual journey has reached another resting point in his life. He should use this time

XIV TEMPERANCE

wisely, so that he may draw upon his own hidden resources and spiritual awareness. Harmony, balance, and patience are of the essence now, to enable us to heighten our own intuition. Some of us find it very hard to be patient in today's fast-moving world. Inwardly we may know the right moment to advance, yet we may feel the need to rush into things. Meditation would be beneficial now; learn to be as the unicorn, for he is spiritually at one with himself.

DIVINATORY MEANING: When the Temperance card appears in the spread, it is important that you do nothing at this time about your situation. You must first learn to be patient; you have no option but to bide time. Timing is of the utmost importance if success is to be assured. This can be applied to many different areas of the reading; for instance, if one is inquiring about health, the reply is "everything in moderation," including eating and drinking. It would be beneficial to give up smoking and start exercising. If financial matters are the focal point, the advice is to tighten your belt and keep a grip of the purse strings. Remember in all cases that patience is a virtue!

REVERSED MEANING: Temperance, spiritual card of patience, turns into the opposite when reversed, representing impatience, impulsiveness, and over-reaction. You must learn to go with the flow now, instead of wasting time and effort trying swim against the tide. If in doubt, do nothing. If you force the issue now, it could bring a disastrous outcome. Instead of rushing, be as the pure white unicorn, still and patient.

XV The Devil

The Devil card portrays a young girl and unicorn gelding, both in shameful submission to the lustful evil powers of the Devil. The unicorn and the girl seem powerless to do anything about their imprisonment. They are suspended in no-man's land, appearing to have nowhere to run.

The Devil himself is a menacing-looking beast, part human, part animal, with long black claws. It is possible that the girl could have escaped this terrible ordeal if she had not succumbed to her basic animal instincts. She should have listened to the higher spiritual guidance of the unicorn, who has remained by her side in her time of woe, ever faithful. In the beginning, the unicorn was attracted by the young girl's virtue and beauty. Theirs was a higher spiritual love; but under the seductive guise of a young man, the Devil seduced the girl, corrupting her honor. The unicorn tried to stop them but the girl went against her better judgment, so now both suffer while the Devil laughs. He sees them as easy prey, for they are prisoners of the Devil because they gave in to their weaknesses. If they were to be strong, they could rise above all this and easily escape.

We all have weaknesses and a touch of the Devil in us, but we must be strong so that we too do not succumb to our lower selves, thereby making ourselves prisoners of our own actions. **DIVINATORY MEANING:** When the Devil appears in the spread it is a strong indication of a shake-up or troubles. This could result in wallowing in self-pity. There is no easy way out of this situation. Although temptation may be put in the way of clear vision, extreme caution is called for.

XV THE DEVIL

If the card of the Lovers is nearby, it may transpire that there is temptation to become involved in a love affair. Taking action on this affair would be disastrous. If you're asking about material considerations (such as home or money), the Devil indicates disruptive influences leading to loss if great care is not taken.

REVERSED MEANING: When the Devil card is reversed, it lessens the negativity of this card, indicating that you are more able to conquer any weaknesses, including addictions to drinking, smoking, gambling, or drug abuse. Light is at the end of the tunnel now, as the spiritual unicorn gathers the strength to bring you out of this stagnation period.

XVI The Tower

The Tower card is depicted by a large stone monument of a unicorn tower. Explosions coming from the unicorn's horn create tumbling rubble and shaky foundations. From this picture we can see that the disruption has caused two people to lose their footing. One man is already lying motionless on the ground as if dead. The other person is falling from the tower to his fate.

This catastrophe may have been caused by such unforeseen disruptive natural forces as earthquakes and volcanoes. Sometimes these occurrences happen without any forewarning. Therefore, the Tower card indicates shaky foundations of either a physical or spiritual nature, meaning discord, upset, and the possibility of being in an unsettled situation where you seem powerless to do anything. Again we go back to the Fool on his journey through life. Some episodes in life just have to be! We all experience upsets to a greater or lesser degree – they are character-building. Although it may seem cruel that life puts us through trials from time to time, we learn from our experiences, hopefully becoming more wise and worldly.

DIVINATORY MEANING: When the Tower card appears in the spread, you need to be prepared for a shake-up in your life. Depending on the surrounding cards, you will be able to determine in exactly which area of your life the upset will take place. For example, if the Tower is surrounded by the eight or ace of pentacles, a sudden unexpected turn of events could lead to more money or a better position in work. If, however, the surrounding cards are cups (emotions), the shake-up could concern relationships.

XVI THE TOWER

REVERSED MEANING: You are now aware of what isn't working out in your life, having already experienced upset or discord. Now is the time when you have to come to terms with what you cannot change and what you can change in your life, but you need to differentiate between the two in order to clear the way to follow your Spiritual path toward the future.

XVII The Star

The Star card depicts a beautiful, virtuous young woman, kneeling down by the deepest blue healing waters. At one time the water in this river was not safe to drink, but the young unicorn, who is pure in body and soul, cleansed the water with his magical horn. The power of the unicorn's horn is so strong that not only does he cleanse and bless the water, he also has the spiritual ability of purification, rendering the water full of healing properties.

The Lady of the Star pours water into the river from her pitcher. She looks wistfully into the glistening water, as if she were wishing for her dreams to come true. Behind her shines a Star so bright it illuminates the land, granting wishes for the pure of heart. This spiritual card portrays the higher spiritual side of ourselves, suggesting that we should learn to draw upon our own psychic powers of intuition so we may be guided by the light. Believe in yourself and the power of the mind. If you can visualize your dreams, you can make them come true.

DIVINATORY MEANING: When the Lady of the Star is with you, she brings the spiritual unicorn into your soul. You can expect something wonderful to happen in the near future as there is a very optimistic outlook now. Dreams really can

XVII THE STAR

become reality; the surrounding cards determine in which area this good fortune will manifest itself. If the question concerns finances or work, surrounded by other positive cards the Star indicates a possible windfall. Whatever your desire, this card suggests a dream come true.

REVERSED MEANING: The implications are rather negative. Hopes are dashed, dreams have not come true. You may feel very disappointed or disillusioned with the situation pertaining to your circumstances. Think more positively about the situation in order to overcome your disappointment. You also need to believe in yourself, as your self-esteem is probably very low. On our journey through life, it is inevitable that things do not always work out the way we want them to. Life is full of ups and downs, but we get over them in time. Tomorrow is another day!

XVIII The Moon

The Moon card symbolizes emotional unsettlement. A minstrel in the picture is gently strumming his mandolin in an attempt to woo the woman, who stands with her hand on her hip, looking quite unsettled. She doesn't feel as though she is in complete control of the situation. She is compelled by the spiritual unicorn and the full moon, and drawn by the soothing music, but she is prone to mood swings (symbolizing woman's emotions being turned upside down). On the ground, a crayfish has crawled out of his dark pool to see what is going on. This dark mysterious creature represents our own hidden suspicions or insecurities, the things that can sometimes play on our mind. The unicorn, rearing up at the full

XVIII THE MOON

moon, displays spiritual awareness and a completion to an experience that could be spiritually enlightening.

DIVINATORY MEANING: When the Moon card appears in the spread, it symbolizes subconscious feelings becoming confused by other emotional disturbances. You may be feeling insecure about a situation and cannot trust your own judgment now. You need to tread very carefully so as not to make a blunder. In time there will be light at the end of the tunnel, and you will know where you stand.

REVERSED MEANING: The situation may be more serious when this card appears reversed. There could be an indication of drug abuse or alcoholism, in an attempt at escapism. This placing also indicates an untrustworthy person who has malicious tendencies and may deliberately deceive you. Be warned to watch those around you and to tread carefully when dealing with people, as someone may have it in for you.

XIX The Sun

The Sun signifies joy and happiness, pictured here by two young people contentedly caressing each other. Meanwhile, the beautiful white unicorn, symbol of purity and spirituality, proudly stands on the hilltop looking at the bright sunshine, representing fulfillment and success. The Fool has traveled far and experienced many things; he has become wise and consequently achieves inner fulfillment and self-realization. The Fool has accomplished what he set out to do; he has attained his goal. The unicorn reminds us of our spiritual selves and the essence of life. The Sun is God's life-giving force, for without it we would surely perish.

XIX THE SUN

DIVINATORY MEANING: Success, fulfillment, and attainment of goals is the message of this card. The surrounding cards will shed light on the area of life most fulfilling for you now. If cups surround, then security in relationships is assured; if the four of rods is close by, marriage could be in the air. This card represents a joyful outcome to situations pertaining to a promotion, a new job, a better standard of living, health, wealth, and happiness.

REVERSED MEANING: Has success already occurred for you? It is possible that you expect everything to fall into your lap, or success may have gone to your head, resulting in a superior attitude that will most certainly bring you down soon. If success has not already occurred, it may be telling you that you are so pessimistic that you are your own worst enemy. As with the reversed Strength card, the Sun can also mean illness. Look at the other cards around it carefully to assess its true meaning.

XX Judgment

The High Priestess is in Judgment as she rises up from the ground with her arms outstretched as if to give praise to the powers that be. She possesses great insight and knowledge of the supernatural, with the ability to perform miracles to bring about joyful resurrection. At each side of her, she has conjured up unicorns who are attracted by her virtue. They rear up on their hind legs as if to salute her and obey her every command.

And so the Fool is almost at the end of his journey. He is now awakened to his higher self, and is well-balanced with a

XX JUDGMENT

good sense of Judgment. He faces the decision of reincarnation or moving up to a higher plane: the choice is his reward.

DIVINATORY MEANING: When Judgment appears in the spread, you must first determine if you are in judgment of the present situation or if, in fact, you are being judged by others. Either way, this is a positive card. In real life, it can indicate legal matters coming out in one's favor. Reflect upon the events leading up to this moment to learn the lessons of your karmic path. Accept that a positive new cycle in your life is about to begin.

REVERSED MEANING: Poor judgment is likely at this time. If you have a decision to make, you must be warned to proceed with great caution. It would benefit you to listen to the spiritual advice of a higher person who knows the ways of the unicorn and the inner self. If this pertains to legal matters, the case may be lost and disappointment will be the result. You may have to backtrack to find out where you went wrong in order to correct your mistakes.

XXI The World

The spiritual woman dances with the unicorn. She holds the World in her hand. We have now come full circle, and the Fool has chosen to begin his journey on a higher path; as is the beginning, so is the end. Everything in life must come full circle. The woman in this picture has learned to listen to the inner voice of the unicorn and dances to a distant tune. Together they can rise above the material plane and are able to see everything in a clearer perspective.

This card indicates our higher selves and our ability to rise above any situation that may have held us back. (Like the Phoenix, we may rise from the ashes and leave them behind.) There will be many decisions to be made in our futures, and travel may be one of them. This placing can indicate distant lands; connections with foreign places are well-aspected. The worldly unicorn is telling us to expect change, and the time scale is within twelve months.

DIVINATORY MEANING: When the World appears in the spread it is foretelling changes, whether they are of a physical nature or simply the way you are viewing your situation. You may have a new or different way of looking at things now, as a result of the experiences you have been through. The World can indicate travel, especially if surrounded by the Chariot or other travel cards. If the two of pentacles is near, a decision connected with finance may be faced in the near future – the outcome will be positive, as long as you listen to your instincts.

XXI THE WORLD

REVERSED MEANING: When the World appears this way, it is warning of loss if great care isn't employed when tying up loose ends. This is symbolic of change in one's life. You have come full circle in life and must draw upon acquired wisdom in order to do what must be done. The problem is, you may not be able to see your situation in a clear perspective, and must be warned to proceed with great care.

Chapter 4

The Minor Arcana

The Minor Arcana consists of 56 cards split into four suits: cups, rods, swords, and pentacles (like the hearts, clubs, spades, and diamonds that you find in playing cards). These cards are numbered similarly to the cards that you would find in a normal deck of playing cards, beginning with ace, two, three, and on up to ten, then followed by page, knight, queen, king. The resemblance to playing cards stems from the old days when it is believed that the tarot was actually invented for playing games, and that in fact they were the forerunner to the ordinary playing cards of today.

Although the tarot is split into two, i.e., the Major Arcana and the Minor Arcana, the Minor Arcana is not less important that the Major Arcana. The Major Arcana pertains to the strong forces that we experience in our lives, such as birth, love, law of the lands, and death. However, the Minor Arcana fills in the details to give us a clearer picture of the future. You would find it quite difficult to be precise in your reading with only half the tarot deck. Although it can be done, I personally feel that it is far more productive to use the full 78 cards.

Court Cards and their Meanings

The court cards are divided into four figures: the page, knight, queen, and king. They represent either a person who may have a strong influence on the inquirer or certain characteristics in the inquirer's life that may affect his or her current situation.

The Pages

The pages usually represent a young person, male or female, from birth up to the mid-twenties. The page signifies youthful expressions and sometimes immaturity, and may not always represent a person. Instead it can indicate messages and news, as pages were the messengers of the court centuries ago.

The Knights

The gallant knights represent a male from mid-twenties to late thirties in years, signifying either the inquirer himself and his own characteristics, or representing a male of relevant description having a strong bearing in the inquirer's life. It may also be telling us that in order to succeed, we need to bring out our more masculine sides.

The Queens

The queens represent a woman over the age of twenty-five. This could be the inquirer or a woman who bears an influence in the inquirer's life. Sometimes (depending on the surrounding cards) it may mean that certain characteristics of our feminine nature need to be nurtured. The queens can also be seen as the maternal cards of the tarot.

The Kings

The kings represent a mature male from late thirties onwards. The kings are the father figures of the tarot. They can represent authoritative figures in everyday life.

THE SUIT OF CUPS

Ace of Cups

The ace is depicted by a single golden chalice overflowing with water (emotions). This is the card of celebration. It is the Cup of Life, bringing celebration and joy into the hearts of people. Three baby unicorns are emerging out of the blue waters of the chalice. This is how unicorns are born. One must open one's heart, for it is the miracle of life. Water trickles down the chalice, resembling tears of joy.

DIVINATORY MEANING: The ace of cups indicates the opportunity for a new love, particularly if the Lovers card is nearby. It is an uplifting card, signifying an emotional reason to celebrate. The new love could be a soulmate. Love is also indicated by the presence of the two of cups, three of cups, and ten of cups, all of which bring some form of emotional happiness in their own right. If the Empress is close by, the celebration could be a birth.

REVERSED MEANING: When you tip a chalice upside down, all the water falls out. So it is with emotions. You may be letting your emotions rule your head, rushing headlong into something that may not be good for you or even be what you expected. This card indicates delays or an off/on situation that requires patience if things are ever going to take off.

Two of Cups

In this picture of the two of cups, we see two young people (man and woman) clinking their chalices together as though they are toasting each other. They appear to be in a great hall, framed by two marble pillars. Standing in front of them is a young unicorn foal, symbolic of purity, showing us that this is a special one-to-one relationship. They are soulmates, their destinies are meant to touch each other, and they are truly compatible.

DIVINATORY MEANING: When this card appears in a spread, it is a strong indication that a special someone has a strong influence over you. You could be experiencing intense true love, particularly if the Lovers are near this card. If the question is one of business, then a partnership could be in the works. Listen to the sound advice from loved ones or close friends before making decisions in financial matters for now.

REVERSED MEANING: When this card appears reversed it may indicate a minor dispute or lover's tiff. There is a slight possibility of a split-up for a short period of time, but this should be seen as more of a cooling-off period rather than anything more serious. Once again, the surrounding cards will help you to determine if this emotional upset is more serious, or if it is indeed just a lover's spat.

If the five of cups is near this card it could be an indication of unreciprocated love leading to disappointment.

ACE OF CUPS

TWO OF CUPS

THREE OF CUPS

FOUR OF CUPS

Three of Cups

Three young women toast each other while standing on the balcony of the great hall. Beautiful blue skies outside depict a calm, peaceful atmosphere. Two young unicorn foals stand to the forefront of the picture. The male stands in the background, and gently caresses the mare in front of him.

DIVINATORY MEANING: There is most certainly a reason to celebrate in the near future. What sort of celebration it will be is suggested by the surrounding cards. If the Lovers card is close, wedding bells are in the air. If the knight of cups is near, expect an invitation coming your way soon. Attend the event – don't be a party pooper!

REVERSED MEANING: There is a danger that you may have a tendency to over-indulge yourself in frivolous activities that may not do you any good. If the seven of cups is nearby, there is a tendency for alcoholism or other over-indulgences in order to escape from certain problems that need to be faced. If other negative cards surround (particularly the Empress reversed, the Devil, or the Tower), frivolity could end in unplanned pregnancy or other personal problems connected with promiscuity.

Four of Cups

Here we see a young man clearly unsettled in his thoughts. He has a decision to make, but he does not know which cup to choose. There has already been an offer out of the blue (as depicted by the angel in the background). Yet this offer may not have been a solid one; instead it was full of promises and dreams of aspirations.

The all-knowing, spiritually guided unicorn knows which cup he would choose; he is quite clearly trying to point the right cup out to his master.

DIVINATORY MEANING: This placing brings with it a feeling of disappointment or dissatisfaction. Consult the surrounding cards to determine the source of unhappiness. It could be disappointment with work or a relationship gone wrong. Yet all hope is not lost. In fact, you haven't quite clearly seen the cup (opportunity) that the unicorn is pointing out.

REVERSED MEANING: As we are dealing with cups, chances are that we are considering relationships. With the reversal of this card, you may have already spotted the unforeseen opportunity and are now feeling motivated enough to make things work out. This could pertain to a previous relationship that you once found boring. Now you can see this relationship in a new light and realize its true value.

Five of Cups

An emotional man stands by a stream. He appears to be keeping his feelings bottled up inside. Yet he is looking longingly at the three cups that have fallen over. Emotions have been spilled. It is plain to see there is great sadness here. We must learn not to cry over spilled milk, what is done is done – and life goes on. In the background we see an older, wiser unicorn who is trying to show us that two cups still stand, and there is still hope for the future.

DIVINATORY MEANING: It is clear from the presence of this card in a spread that disappointment is in your heart. Shut the door on the past and look to the opportunities that lay ahead. The experiences that have led to this unhappiness happened for a reason; and although that reason may not seem apparent at the present moment, you will eventually find that you have learned something valuable.

REVERSED MEANING: The upset may now be a thing of the past. No one ever said that life was going to be easy; one must learn to take the rough with the smooth. You have learned to come to terms with that, and you're ready to put this painful emotional experience behind you now. Listen to the advice of the unicorn. Pick up the two remaining cups and makes the most of what you have. With this acceptance, you will be rewarded with spiritual growth. Something good is in store!

Six of Cups

This card depicts children playing quite contentedly on the grass, with a young unicorn foal watching over them and keeping them safe from harm. The enchanted palace stands in the background – they play near the security of home and familiar surroundings. This card is reminiscent of childhood, bringing us back to our past. However, it can also be seen as looking ahead; for as we were once children ourselves, perhaps we shall, in turn, have children of our own one day.

DIVINATORY MEANING: To get a clear reading, you must first take into consideration the cards that surround this situation. If your query is in connection with family matters, it may indicate that children play a big part in your life and

FIVE OF CUPS

SIX OF CUPS

SEVEN OF CUPS

EIGHT OF CUPS

decisions at present. On the other hand, if you are asking about friends, then it is possible that an old friend from the past may be in touch; this could lead to a reunion, especially if the ten of cups is nearby.

REVERSED MEANING: You have a tendency to live in the past. You must stop going over and over things, as you are only hurting yourself. If the five of cups is next to this card then it is possible that you may be thinking about getting back with a former lover. This may not be a good idea. Look to the future now, putting the past behind you for your own peace of mind.

Seven of Cups

This card is truly magical and mystical. In the basement of the castle, the Magus is full of imagination. He has conjured up several cups, each containing something different. This magical man has a slightly warped sense of humor, for the cups do not all possess nice things. A small demon perches on one cup, while a dragon comes out of another. These signify one's worst fears or nightmares. The other cups hold coins, diamonds, and dolphins, and are significant of our aspirations. The highest aspirations of all are represented by the unicorn, emerging from the front cup. The Magus holds in his hand the sands of time in an hourglass.

DIVINATORY MEANING: This card pertains to hopes and fears. Whether you are positive or negative in your thinking at the moment will depend on the cards around this one. It is possible that your thinking is confused and that you are not too sure what the best move might be. Where a big decision is concerned, you need to wait to see what happens in the near future. Find a positive outlet, such as drawing or writing, for frustrated creativity.

REVERSED MEANING: You are beginning to see things in a clearer light now. You have got your priorities in clear perspective, and are not allowing emotions cloud your better judgment as you did before.

Eight of Cups

The eight of cups depicts a man about to venture across the stepping stones that cross the fast flowing stream. He is leaving his unicorn on the bank and is about to turn his back on a particular situation. He doesn't look upset about what he is doing; he has already collected eight cups, so he feels it is time to explore a new direction in order to continue learning. The unicorn also seems to be having a change of heart – but will he stay, or follow his friend?

DIVINATORY MEANING: As the man in the picture is making his way across the stream on his own, you may also feel alone for a while, especially if any negative cards surround this, such as the three of swords (separation). This may be a time to experience the next phase of learning on your own. If the question pertains to a relationship, then it is likely that you are experiencing a change of heart and realizing that most good things must come to an end. However, do not become too disillusioned, because "what you lose on the roundabouts, you gain on the swings."

REVERSED MEANING: You may have deep-rooted insecurities that prevent you from being able to make a firm commitment. You may be frightened of becoming too close to someone. You must learn to trust again if you want to find complete happiness and contentment. If your question is connected to education, you must understand in order to attain goals and achieve recognition.

Nine of Cups

This card portrays a mature man who seems to be quite content with all he surveys. By his side, a unicorn peacefully rests after his hard day of travel and work. He has earned this rest. High up in the sky, an eagle soars.

In the course of our lives, as we learn to be more spiritual we also learn to rise above the everyday activities that bring us down, much as the eagle rises and soars above the earth. We can all too easily lose touch with our spiritual selves. The cups are all stacked up, reminding us of completion and the fulfillment of dreams.

DIVINATORY MEANING: This card certainly indicates fulfillment of wishes; however, you can't see if the cups are full or empty. This means that although one goal may have been reached, peace and contentment may not be long-lasting. Look at the surrounding cards to find out what this is pertaining to. If it is love, and some of the remaining cards are not too positive, it is possible that the thrill was in setting the goal and not attaining it. Now that that's accomplished – what next?

REVERSED MEANING: Although this card is reversed, it does not necessarily follow that the interpretation would read "all hopes are lost." However, there is a strong possibility that there will be delays in attaining a goal. You must take into account the surrounding cards to ascertain if in fact you are trying to reach too far too soon. You won't get what you want immediately. You have to be more realistic in your hopes and dreams if you really want to succeed.

Ten of Cups

This card depicts happiness, contentment, happy endings, true love that is both deep and spiritual. A man and a woman stand in each other's arms watching a child frolicking on green pastures with a young unicorn. Above is rainbow of golden chalices, pointing toward good things to come. The feeling of happiness and tranquility is strong.

DIVINATORY MEANING: This powerful card represents harmony and true love. Surrounded by other positive cups, it will act like the Lovers card of the Major Arcana. Representing true spiritual love, it does not necessarily mean love of a sexual nature. It could relate to close friends or a platonic relationship. You know how to give and take, thus you are able to give love and receive love in return. It is the card of happy families, offering love, support, security, and a bright future.

REVERSED MEANING: When this card appears reversed, it can be an indication of squabbles and misunderstandings. Look to this relationship now and try to smooth things over in order to prevent the situation from getting even worse. Try to find out why there is a breakdown in communication. At worst, the card reversed could predict signs of incompatibility that were not apparent in this relationship before. Take into consideration the surrounding cards in order to decipher what the outcome might be.

NINE OF CUPS

TEN OF CUPS

PAGE OF CUPS

KNIGHT OF CUPS

Page of Cups

Keep in mind that pages usually represent messengers. This card depicts a young adolescent (male or female) dressed in a dark brown tunic, similar to how messengers of the court dressed in bygone years. The youth holds a chalice up high as if to propose a toast to the unicorn, who is obviously quite elated. The stallion stands proud and regal in the great hall. In the background is a large pillar shaped like a unicorn's horn. Reminiscent of a carousel, their dance gives off an air of happiness and jubilation.

DIVINATORY MEANING: When this card appears in a spread, it indicates news of emotional happiness or an invitation (social message). It could also be referring to a young person in your life (up to age 25). If positive cards surround this card, such as the four of rods, it means news of a forthcoming celebration, a gathering of family and friends, or even a marriage. If the two or three of swords surround this card, it suggests a separation.

REVERSED MEANING: When this card appears reversed it may indicate hold-ups and delays in communication. Perhaps you are waiting to hear news of a friend, but this is a slow period and this news will not travel fast. Socially speaking, you would benefit from spending a little more time on your own instead of socializing.

Knight of Cups

The knight of cups is a very proud and handsome young man. He sits astride the unicorn's back, full of feeling, with a cup in his right hand. He sports a broad-brimmed hat with a large feather in it. A gallant knight, he is admired by many for his honest, open approach to life. The ladies can't help but falling in love with him. Being a water sign, he is warm, emotional, and understanding. His unicorn is an excellent listener, eager to leap to his defense when necessary. Again in the background we see the unicorn horn pillars that suggest the magic of old-fashioned carousels.

DIVINATORY MEANING: You must first decide if this card represents you or if it represents a man in your life. The knight of cups is a gallant young man, usually medium- to fair-haired, and is symbolic of a water sign (Pisces, Cancer, Scorpio). If this is not his actual birth sign, you will find that he portrays the characteristics of the water-sign male. If surrounded by the Lovers, the indication from this card is a proposal of marriage, or any other proposal of an emotional nature.

REVERSED MEANING: When this card appears reversed it is not so negative but depicts a charming man with all the attraction of the water signs. However, he is more of a "gigolo" who falls in and out of love very easily, leaving hearts broken, because for all his charms he is frightened of commitment and never keeps his word.

Queen of Cups

Pictured on a royal blue background, the queen of cups is a highly emotional lady. She always looks for the best in everyone; yet some take advantage of her kind-heartedness and do not always appreciate her as they should. Like the Empress in the Major Arcana, this queen is also a maternal figure. She is romantic, caring, and very protective toward her loved ones. She can be a bit of a dreamer, not even noticing the presence of the unicorn, who has been lured by her virtue.

DIVINATORY MEANING: The queen of cups is a very motherly, loving, and giving woman, one whom you could turn to for comfort. If the queen of cups does not represent you, then she is one who plays an important role in your life: a mother, wife, lover, or true friend that you could turn to in confidentiality. She draws upon her feminine intuition to advise – quite often she is a person who has psychic abilities.

REVERSED MEANING: As she is like water sign women (Pisces, Cancer, or Scorpio), she is very emotional, too much so at times. She may let her emotions rule her head, and needs to be encouraged to see things in a clear perspective to avoid being hurt. The queen of cups reversed is too soft-hearted, a sucker for a sob story. It is very easy for someone to play on her emotions. She must toughen up for her own good, and stop living her life around what everyone else wants. She leaves herself wide open to be taken advantage of and used.

QUEEN OF CUPS

KING OF CUPS

King of Cups

This monarch is a warm, fatherly man who you could turn to him in your hour of need and he would be a great protector. As a mature water sign man, he is very deep in his passions, but is secretive and does not always show his true feelings. His unicorn also gives an air of intensity and mystery. Although unicorns are generally placid and affectionate, they are also protective of their loved ones. If they sense danger, their emotions rise within, urging them to fight to the end for their masters.

DIVINATORY MEANING: The king of cups is a mature man who could be described as being deep and secretive but trustworthy. He may represent you, but if not, he is a man who has a strong influence in your life or situation: a father, husband, close friend, or lover. He cares deeply, he is emotionally sensitive (water sign), and is a good confidante.

REVERSED MEANING: As with the previous card, the king can also be over-emotional. Here we find the negative side of Scorpio emerging. Outwardly he may appear to be strong and in control of his life, but inwardly he may turn to drink to drown his problems because he feels he can't cope. He may find it hard to let go, which makes him possessive and even jealous at times. Be strong in order to overcome emotional problems, or you will end up being your own worst enemy or bringing about your own downfall. Try to figure out what is eating away at you; it may be a separation in your life. Be more positive about the future instead of being skeptical all the time. If the Temperance card is close, the message is everything in moderation, including drinking or other vices.

THE SUIT OF SWORDS

Ace of Swords

The ace of swords is depicted on a lilac background (lilac is the spiritual color). The sword stands out strongly as the main feature in this picture. The wreath around the top of the sword is the crowning glory, evincing victory and strength. On each side of the sword are two small, winged unicorns, symbolizing magical influences. As the victorious sword may sever ties or bring a situation to an end, the unicorns depict spiritual love, birth, and fresh beginnings. There is a triumphant feeling to this card, as intense energy flows into determination, ultimately leading to victory.

DIVINATORY MEANING: The ace of swords can be seen as victory over problems that you may have been facing recently, signifying the end of a difficult phase. Look at the cards surrounding this one to determine if it is victory over a personal problem, or if you are severing ties with someone in order to let new beginnings occur. If the question pertains to finances, it may mean a change of job or a financial income coming to an end. Surrounded by negative cards such as Death or the Tower, it means a death or bereavement of some kind.

REVERSED MEANING: The ace of swords reversed is an indication of frustrations and setbacks. You may be trying to force a situation, and if you are not careful, you may lose everything. Learn to be more patient, or else you will suffer a loss, or situations will backfire if you are too forceful in your approach. If you are asking a "yes or no" question, the answer with this card is definitely no!

ACE OF SWORDS

TWO OF SWORDS

THREE OF SWORDS

FOUR OF SWORDS

Two of Swords

A woman stands between two unicorns, holding a sword in each hand, and with her eyes closed, as though she is confused and does not know which way to turn. This woman clearly faces a big decision in her life; she is imprisoned in her own situation. The scene is one of duality: castle turrets on either side, unicorns almost mirror images of each other. Which way will she turn? (Look at the surrounding cards to find the answer.)

DIVINATORY MEANING: When the two of swords appears in your spread, it is a warning that you may not be able to see things in a clear perspective. You feel as though you are at a standstill, unable to see a way out. Your situation may seem hopeless to you, but as with everything negative, you must always have hope.

If you are asking about health matters, it is likely that there will be suffering with women's troubles, especially if the queen of cups is nearby, or if the ace of cups or Empress cards appear reversed. If this card is near the three of swords or the Devil, there is a strong indication of separation. If the Judgment card is near, then it can indicate divorce. There is a strong possibility that a big decision needs to be made soon, relating to any one of these areas.

REVERSED MEANING: The two of swords is kinder when it appears reversed in a spread. The indication is more calm after troubled waters. Differences will be resolved and harmony will reign once more. If the question is one of relationships, then it is likely that although this is a difficult relationship, both parties have learned to give and take for the sake of resolution.

Three of Swords

The picture of the three of swords is set within the castle walls. It portrays a young couple who have turned their backs on each other. From their body language, we can see the woman feels very insecure, folding her arms across herself for comfort. The man looks as though he feels their relationship is over, and does not know what to do or say to make things right. Something has come between them, maybe a third person, or in this case, maybe the woman's love for her unicorn. The poor unicorn walks away in this picture, appearing emotionally hurt, blaming himself for the couple's upset, although he was an innocent party.

None of the three beings in this picture seem to notice the three swords hanging on the wall, signifying fate. We all find it easier to pin the blame on someone else, even when the situation is a result of the natural course of life and no one may be at fault.

DIVINATORY MEANING: When the three of swords appears in your spread it indicates heartache and misery; if related to relationships, there may be more going on than meets the eye. Two is company, three is a crowd. With the Devil, Judgment, Death, or four of rods close by, then the relationship has definitely come to an end, leaving you feeling devastated. A feeling of grief is often common with this card, although a death as such does not always have to occur. The death of a marriage, of course, leaves a feeling of emptiness. If the question relates to health, then the indications are of heart trouble, although not necessarily death. Again, you need to take the surrounding cards into account.

REVERSED MEANING: The negativities are lessened when this card appears reversed. It is a sign of recovery from illness or emotional heartache. You have been through a very difficult time in your life, but now you realize that maybe everything is for the best in the end, even if you still bear the emotional scars. You are on the mend and much more able to cope with life.

Four of Swords

The setting for this card is a bed chamber somewhere within a castle. The knight looks as if he is recuperating after a long, hard battle. The room he is in seems very stark with its cold stone floor and nothing more than a stone slab to rest his weary head upon. It gives one the impression of a chapel of rest.

Four swords hang high on the wall, signifying that forces beyond the knight's control have brought him to a standstill. His faithful unicorn lies by his side; he, too, is weary and in need of a well-earned rest.

DIVINATORY MEANING: The four of swords pertains to enforced rest. Time is needed for one to recover completely. The surrounding cards will pinpoint whether this pertains to physical or emotional rest. If the eight of swords or Tower cards are prominent, then enforced rest may come in the form of hospitalization. If you tend to be rather headstrong and are inclined to be a "work-a-holic," then the tarot is warning you that if you don't slow down or make better use of your time, your mind may say "I can't stop now" but your body will collapse. You will have only yourself to blame.

Keep in mind that this need for rest could pertain to someone close to you, rather than to yourself.

REVERSED MEANING: This card signifies a recuperation period; the more positive cards surrounding this, the greater the chance of full recovery. If you are asking about work, the indications are that after a period of enforced rest (probably through circumstances beyond your control, such as ill health or being dismissed from a job) you are now fighting fit and raring to go!

Five of Swords

The five of swords portrays a warrior with a sword in each hand. He has just finished battling with his enemies, but is still prepared to face any adversary that may stand in his way in the future. His unicorn stands unfettered by his side, as if to give moral support.

However, in the background, two devious enemies are discussing the recent events. They are plotting and scheming against the warrior, but it is unlikely their plan will succeed as they are spineless characters of no substance.

DIVINATORY MEANING: When the five of swords appears in the spread, there is a threat of jealousy coming from a vindictive enemy. You may be in a back-biting situation that could cause a lot of upset. From reading the surrounding cards, you must try to deduce where this treachery is coming from, and who (if anyone) you can trust. Sometimes this can indicate trouble from an enemy resurfacing from the past. You must not antagonize any situation that could (figuratively) blow up in your face.

REVERSED MEANING: When this card appears reversed, jealousy and upset are behind you. You will enjoy victory over personal problems; you will now be cleared of any malicious gossip or slanderous rumors brought about by jealous people who are intent upon bringing about your downfall.

Six of Swords

A warrior stands in a long boat with a punt in his hand. He must sail above adversity in order to reach a place of peace. In the distance, a solitary unicorn proudly stands on a high, snow-capped cliff. He is the great prince of this land, commanding respect and harmony; he is loved and worshiped by all. The traveler's boat is stacked with swords for his protection. His clever plan for protection could rebound on him – when he hits troubled waters, the rocking of his boat could cause the swords to pierce the bottom, making the boat sink.

DIVINATORY MEANING: You have been going through a very difficult, stressful time, but sometimes we have to experience difficulties in order to learn and grow. This way, hopefully, we don't make the same mistakes twice. If surrounding cards look bright, the outlook is optimistic as troubles gradually become a thing of the past. If the Chariot is reversed near this card, the warning could be trouble with travel or vehicles.

REVERSED MEANING: You must be very careful not to fall into the same trap twice. It is likely that your judgment is impaired in some way, and you don't listen to logic. Your own course of actions could take you right back to square one. Avoid creating turmoil, for you are the one who will lose in the end.

Seven of Swords

The seven of swords portrays a "thief in the night" scene. The warrior is fleeing with four swords, as well as his own sword in his right hand, and two swords planted in the ground behind him. The scene indicates treachery and deceit, as this devious man smirks to himself with a false sense of victory. However, his acts have been observed by the all-seeing, all-knowing unicorn.

DIVINATORY MEANING: The seven of swords in the spread warns of a tricky situation in which you stand to lose if you are not careful. As with the five of swords, jealousy may be present. Be aware of underhanded people working behind the scenes to bring turmoil and disruption into your life. This is the card of treachery and deceit; one must guard property and valuable belongings, especially if the Devil card is nearby.

REVERSED MEANING: When this negative card is reversed it lessens the problems otherwise indicated, bringing triumph over personal vendettas. It is possible that what was once lost or taken will now be rightfully returned.

Eight of Swords

The eight of swords portrays a solemn woman, who looks lost in the cold snow, imprisoned by swords. Her only companion is the young unicorn, but even this magical beast seems unsure about which way to turn. The eight swords surrounding the woman are the cause of her anxiety, and there appears to be no way out of this predicament. She stands on barren land, not a soul to come to her rescue.

FIVE OF SWORDS

SIX OF SWORDS

SEVEN OF SWORDS

EIGHT OF SWORDS

DIVINATORY MEANING: This is a warning to health, property, or emotional happiness. There are limitations and physical restrictions on you when this card appears in the spread. If it is placed near the two of swords, feminine problems may be the trouble. If health is not the question, then you must first decipher if this is portraying a real problem or if in fact you are your own worst enemy. There is a tendency to make matters worse in one's own mind than they really are. You may feel stuck, but only you can change that. Consult the rest of the cards to determine the outcome or solution.

REVERSED MEANING: You have come down to earth with a bump, and realize now that you are antagonizing yourself, imprisoning yourself in your own situation. You must see the way out of this difficulty so you may advance in life instead of feeling stuck in a rut. Find the strength to break free in order to find peace and tranquility once more.

Nine of Swords

A solitary woman dressed in a deep purple velvet gown hangs her head, overwhelmed with sorrow and anxiety. In the background, eight swords point down toward the floor; there is no way out. The ninth sword is lying on the floor at her feet, preventing her from moving forward. A young unicorn foal comes to comfort the woman, but she appears so ensconced in grief that she does not even notice he is there. The room she is in appears cold and bare.

DIVINATORY MEANING: Keeping in mind that swords rule air, and consequently the way in which we think, we see the ultimate in dilemmas when this card appears in a spread.

The problem is that you tend to let worries and inner fears blow out of proportion. Do not lose sight of reality completely. What troubles you so much that you are in danger of literally worrying yourself sick? We know from experience that when we get worked up we become stressed out, creating or at least aggravating health problems. Look for any other indication of health problems in the other cards to decipher the severity of this problem. Maybe you would benefit from consulting a professional with whom you could share your troubles.

REVERSED MEANING: As with the other negative swords reversed, this is a "light at the end of the tunnel" card. You feel able to rise above the problems that have been haunting you. After what has been a long, hard struggle emotionally or a long battle with health, the problems begin to resolve themselves, leaving you feeling much better.

Ten of Swords

The ten of swords depicts a dead man lying on a snow-covered plateau, with two swords protruding from his back. Above him stands the warrior, victorious in his kill. From the sword in the dead man's hand and the remaining swords stuck in the ground surrounding him, we can deduce that a terrible battle has gone on and the poor man has fought to his death. Standing in the snow, a stallion unicorn displays high-spirited anger at this horrific sight.

DIVINATORY MEANING: Unlike the nine of swords, where the concern is an event that may happen in the near future, the ten of swords portrays a negative situation which has already occurred. Therefore you must try to accept the things that you cannot change and learn to make the most of what you have got in order to get over this feeling of defeat as soon as possible. You are over the worst now, and must face the future. This card gives one the feeling of being stabbed in the back or being badly let down. At least this situation is now coming to an end. Look at the surrounding cards to establish what fate has in store for your future.

REVERSED MEANING: After suffering losses or setbacks, you may rest assured that you are now over the worst. The disaster you've experienced is unlikely to ever occur again. It is time to start afresh. The surrounding cards will inform you if the disaster was linked with emotions (cups) or with finances, e.g., ten of pentacles reversed (bankruptcy).

Page of Swords

A young page strolls along a snow-covered pathway. (In real life, this young person could be either male or female.) The magical unicorn eagerly comes to greet the page, to tell him the latest news. The page is very bright and quick-minded. He will learn a lot from his unicorn companion, and eventually will pass on relevant information to those worthy of his wisdom. The page has a long way to go yet, and has great many things to experience. This pathway is only the beginning of his road to knowledge. He ponders the many experiences yet to come.

DIVINATORY MEANING: The page of swords represents a young person, male or female, under the age of twenty-five. This person has all the qualities of an air sign: quick-thinking,

NINE OF SWORDS

TEN OF SWORDS

PAGE OF SWORDS

KNIGHT OF SWORDS

witty, clever, and creative. The page of swords may also be a secret admirer; you should be able to gather this information from the other cards. If this card does not pertain to a person in your life, it may be pointing to the qualities of the air sign needing to be brought out in your own character. The swords pertain to sharp, clear words; you may need some constructive criticism to help gain a clear perspective for the future. Facing the truth will not do you any harm.

REVERSED MEANING: Some people are too quick to criticize, not always choosing their words carefully. This may lead to sharp words, offense being taken, and general discord. Sometimes this card appears reversed in the spread of a parent who is suffering problems with an uncooperative or rebellious teenager.

Knight of Swords

On a serene, snowy plain, a gallant, handsome knight sits high and proud on his unicorn stallion. The knight's sword is raised victoriously in his hand, as though he has just returned from battle. The emblem in the top corners of this royal family of swords is that of a dragon, signifying air and the power of mind. The knight is either an air sign or has air sign qualities, such as cleverness and intelligence, with the gifted ability to be highly versatile.

DIVINATORY MEANING: When this card appears in the spread, it may be representing either you or a person who influences your life. The knight of swords is a medium- to dark-haired man with either green or blue eyes. He possesses strong ideas and a sharp mind. At his best he is a real charmer;

at worst he can be very headstrong, convinced that he is always in the right, and is not easily swayed in his opinions. Intellectually speaking, this card encourages self-assertion. Do not be frightened of speaking out.

REVERSED MEANING: When this card appears reversed, it indicates sharp words. For whatever reason, you may be acting too aggressively or using too much force to attain your goal. If this appears in a woman's spread, there is a threat of violence from an aggressive person connected with her. If the two of swords is near, the aggression may be from an ex-lover or partner who won't let go. Look at the other cards to determine what action should be taken to overcome this situation as quickly as possible.

Queen of Swords

The queen of swords stands alone (but for her unicorn companion) in the snow. She holds her sword in her right hand, indicating strength and self-sufficiency. This woman does not need anyone to help her. However, we can see from her body language that she feels cold and alone. Maybe she has been too forceful in her actions, driving away all those who want to be with her. She is an attractive woman with long, flowing black hair, and although she puts on her brave face, within she feels empty.

DIVINATORY MEANING: This card sometimes portrays a widow, or a woman who lives alone. She is strong-minded and self-sufficient. She does not need anyone to fend for her, as she is more than capable of fending for herself. On the surface, this medium- to dark-haired lady appears very headstrong and efficient. However, when you get to know her she can be a source of inspiration. This card may even portray you. The queen of swords is a very loving person once you get close enough to be able to see beneath the surface.

REVERSED MEANING: When reversed, the swords in this card are a strong indication of a woman with a sharp tongue. She appears to be a hard woman, embittered by life's experiences. She may be tyrannical and full of resentment, a jealous woman who is a vindictive and malicious gossip. She puts up a cold front, but one needs to find out why. If this card portrays you, you must change your attitude toward life and people, for you are too suspicious for your own good. You will not find happiness while you are in this frame of mind.

King of Swords

The king of swords depicts a mature man, worldly in his knowledge. He has dismounted his unicorn, and stands for a moment, surveying his land. This is a very intelligent king – nothing escapes him. He is also very intellectual, philosophically finding a solution for most any problem that may occur. His unicorn represents spiritual intuition. Sometimes it is best to be guided by our inner feelings.

DIVINATORY MEANING: The king of swords represents a mature man in his late thirties or older. He is medium to dark, possibly going gray, with fair eyes. He is extremely clever and wise, usually a professional man: lawyer, doctor, or other professional adviser. He has a quick mind, always learning or improving his skills. If he does not represent you, then he can be seen as an intellectual genius who may be advising

QUEEN OF SWORDS

KING OF SWORDS

you wisely in matters of business, legalities, or health. He is a true professional. It would be wise to bring out these skills within yourself if you want to attain your goals.

REVERSED MEANING: The king of swords reversed has abused his finer qualities. He has become a manipulative, power-hungry person of no moral standing. Beware of a devious, underhanded person who is not adverse to using you for his own gain if need be. He is selfish – a liar and a cheat. In matters concerning the heart, he is unfeeling, even cruel.

THE SUIT OF RODS

Ace of Rods

The ace of rods depicts a large, golden unicorn rod surrounded by three tiny unicorns in flight. The bright rays of golden sunshine begin to fill the skies from behind the stormy clouds that are now dissipated. This signifies the birth of a new venture, or sunshine after the rain.

DIVINATORY MEANING: The ace of rods indicates new beginnings and fresh ideas. The storm clouds in the background that are making way for sunshine encourage you to prepare for a fresh start, as there is now calm after the storm. If you are asking about relationships, this card indicates a fresh start to an emotional situation. You must determine from the other cards if this fresh start means someone new coming on the scene, or merely looking at an old relationship from a new point of view. If you are asking about work, this card indicates opportunities to either branch out or begin something new. In areas concerning health, it can be symbolic of birth.

REVERSED MEANING: When this card appears reversed, you must study the surrounding cards to see what area of your life is suffering from setbacks and delays. If the Fool is close, the indications are less haste, less waste. Near the Sun reversed, it could mean the complete cancellation of a new venture. You need to go back to the drawing board and think again before rushing headlong into things that won't work out due to lack of planning.

Two of Rods

The two of rods depicts a young man dressed in a tunic of a burgundy hue. He has turned his back on one unicorn rod, and holds another in his left hand. In his right hand he holds the world, indicating ultimate satisfaction through the experiences gained in the recent past. He is now contemplating the option of crossing the great spiritual lake that glistens and flows before him. By his side a young unicorn colt gazes across the water, curious to know what is on the other side. The unicorn trusts in his master's decision. This picture signifies a young man turning his back on one situation and looking out toward a new one.

DIVINATORY MEANING: The two of rods signifies lessons have been learned and knowledge gained through communicating with others. Sadly, all good things must come to an end at some time in our lives. This card may indicate that the time has come for change, but through knowing and spending time with someone, you have grown more wise and developed spiritually. As the young man in the picture holds the world in his hand, so it is that the world is yours to experience. If the Chariot is next to this card, travel is likely; if the World card is present also, travel could be across water. If you're asking about relationships, this card signifies the strong possibility of more than one marriage.

REVERSED MEANING: When this card is reversed and next to the three of rods reversed or the two of swords, it is a warning that strong differences of opinion could result in violent outbursts of temper. It would be safer to agree to disagree in this delicate situation.

Three of Rods

A mature man sits on a rock. He is clothed in a burgundy tunic with fur trim boots. His pose gives one the impression that he is deep in thought, planning his next move. He looks longingly toward two spiritual unicorns grazing in the valley. Behind him stand two unicorn staffs, representing his past experiences. In the foreground is a new unicorn staff, indicating the opportunity for fresh starts and new beginnings.

DIVINATORY MEANING: The three of rods indicates the perfection of associations. You may be at a personal crossroads in your life now. Look at your environment to decipher what or who is good for you, and what or who is holding you back. The time has come to "spring clean" your life. Encourage the positive. In matters of relationships, this card may portray "third time lucky" situations. You may have experienced a broken marriage, and now another relationship has fallen apart – yet there are positive signs for happiness in the future with someone new. If the Lovers turn up next to this card, the indication may be a love triangle.

ACE OF RODS

TWO OF RODS

THREE OF RODS

FOUR OF RODS

REVERSED MEANING: This card reversed indicates delays and setbacks due to or connected with other people around you. There could be postponement of a group activity or a creative block in a new enterprise, both leading to frustration. If the question is one of travel, there are likely to be delays, if not cancellations.

Four of Rods

The four of rods depicts two young lovers, under a floral archway; it looks as though they have just sealed their engagement. As a token of the young man's love for the woman, a gift of a beautiful young unicorn has been given. He lies quite still and tranquil at their feet. The pillars supporting the arch are made up of four glistening unicorn staffs. We can see a silhouette of a fairy-tale castle in the background, giving the impression that these lovers are in the garden of spiritual love. The red and white roses are symbolic of spiritual and everlasting love.

DIVINATORY MEANING: The four of rods is a happy card. It is known as the card of marriage, love, and partnerships of all kinds. It brings fulfillment into one's life. This could suggest an invitation to a marriage celebration. If, judging by the other cards, marriage is not in the air, then this could be an indication of a favorable business partnership.

REVERSED MEANING: If the cards surrounding this one are bright, then this is still a positive card when reversed; but it tends to indicate joy, happiness, and love without the commitment of marriage. You may be committed to living with someone. However, if the other cards are negative, the indication is more likely to be different viewpoints existing between partners. If the three of swords or Tower cards also appear in the spread, then a very shaky relationship may dissolve completely.

Five of Rods

The scene is set in an enchanted fairy glade, but the peace and tranquility are broken by two young men who appear to be engrossed in competitive battle, each one determined to beat the other. The unicorn in between them knows that their battle is only horseplay. This excites the young filly to prance about and rear up in anticipation of the outcome.

DIVINATORY MEANING: This is the card of mock battles. Differences of opinion give rise to misunderstandings and fallouts. Silly, trivial matters are blown out of proportion. Be attuned to discord and conflict. You may be working in a back-stabbing environment where you must keep your wits about you in order to survive. This hostile situation is not good for you – the other cards in the spread may offer a solution.

REVERSED MEANING: It is more than likely that you are through your difficult patch. You have vented your anger and all is now calm. You do not feel the need to constantly battle anymore. This card appears quite often after a separation, when all the squabbling has finally come to an end.

Six of Rods

The six of rods brings victory in battle and the ability to over-come problems. Here we see a gallant warrior sitting proudly upon his white stallion unicorn, as if prepared for anything. He is about to set off on a new, more positive venture, full of con-fidence, with his ready supply of rods strapped firmly to him.

DIVINATORY MEANING: The appearance of this card sig-nifies victory over personal problems. Prepare for a new ven-ture or change of direction for the better. If pentacles are in the spread, you will experience financial success. If cups are sur-rounding this card, the indication is emotional happiness, per-haps winning the hand in marriage of the person you love.

REVERSED MEANING: All hopes seem to be shattered and your worst inner fears have come to light. There is a strong feeling of defeat when this card appears reversed in a spread. If Justice or Judgment are also in the spread, the defeat may be a legal one. Pick yourself up and dust yourself off, ready to begin again – put your loss down to experience.

Seven of Rods

The seven of rods portrays a man who holds a unicorn rod high in his hands, a picture of victory. As he is higher than the six unicorn rods in front of him, he is quite clearly in a posi-tion of advantage, ready to fight off any adversaries that may prey upon him. The unicorn by his side is stomping at the ground, ready to defend him.

DIVINATORY MEANING: This is a victory card, especial-ly if the surrounding cards in this spread are positive. In spite

FIVE OF RODS

SIX OF RODS

SEVEN OF RODS

EIGHT OF RODS

of opposition, you have the ability to persevere, winning in the end. You are a survivor, struggling on in the face of adversity, drawing on your inner strength to finally pull through. Always keep in mind that when times are hard, if we just hang in there we will win in the end.

REVERSED MEANING: You must hold on, for you are weary of battle and struggle. You feel weak and vulnerable, but depending on the surrounding cards, you are not defeated yet. Provided you believe in yourself and have the will to survive, there is still a chance.

Eight of Rods

The eight of rods portrays an athletic man alongside his unicorn, holding his bow taught, ready to shoot his arrows through the air. His arrows are carved out of wood into the shape of unicorn horns, indicative of his spiritual swiftness. He is a messenger of good will, and has already shot three unicorn arrows into the future. The other four arrows are standing by his feet, ready for swift dispatch.

DIVINATORY MEANING: This card suggests messages or news traveling toward you; if cups surround, the message is one of love. If pentacles surround this card, the message or news will relate to finances or work. This is a time of growing opportunity, and as with the five of pentacles, the card indicates an "all or nothing" situation. Take what you can now, and make the most of it.

REVERSED MEANING: Messages reversed indicate letters going astray, miscommunication, an attempt to meet someone at a mutually misunderstood meeting place – all leading to frustrations, letdowns, upset, and quarrels. Don't make any important decisions at this time if you can possibly help it, because you may not be able to rely on your own judgment.

Nine of Rods

The nine of rods portrays a man bewildered by the amount of obstructions and problems that he must face. He has barricaded himself in with eight rods. He looks ahead in anticipation of which adversaries may confront him next. He can't even mount his unicorn to escape, for fear of being attacked from behind. This card depicts insecurities, one feeling imprisoned within one's self.

DIVINATORY MEANING: This card indicates you may be feeling as though you stand alone against the world. The message is patience, for it is better to bide your time and remain calm than to fly off the handle and risk losing out. Although you may be feeling stuck, the indications are that you should just wait it out. If in doubt, do nothing. Consider the direction provided by the surrounding cards to determine exactly what makes you feel so insecure. Are you feeling ostracized at work, or are you feeling somewhat rejected in your personal life?

REVERSED MEANING: When this card appears reversed, the opposite applies. Rather than treading cautiously, you are at risk of leaping headlong into something without first planning a strategy. Through impetuosity you may suffer loss or hurt. Think twice before acting on impulse.

Ten of Rods

A mature man is loaded down with rods. He looks as though this burden is almost too great to bear. Looking down toward his feet, he does not notice the unicorn, who looks on as if to say, "You will never make it alone, let me help you." The man has taken on far more than he can comfortably handle. The unicorn is powerless to do anything, as one cannot help a person in need if he will not help himself.

DIVINATORY MEANING: When this card appears in the spread, you are in danger of taking on too much. If you do, you will only succeed in running yourself into the ground. Look at the surrounding cards; if the Magician or the Emperor cards are reversed, you may be abusing your authority and becoming unrealistic, but at the same time you are adamant that you can cope. In this situation, you are bringing about your own downfall.

REVERSED MEANING: The opposite applies when this card appears reversed. You are able to shake off some responsibilities that have been grinding you into the ground. If pentacles are in this spread, the indication is that the workload is not as great as it has been, and you have the opportunity to relax a little now after meeting a deadline. You may be deciding to move from full-time employment to part-time, leaving more time for yourself.

NINE OF RODS

TEN OF RODS

PAGE OF RODS

KNIGHT OF RODS

Page of Rods

A young boy calls out across a vast terrain. The emblem at the top of this card is a phoenix, rising from the ashes, representing fire signs or fire sign characteristics. The boy is desperately trying to beckon the unicorn, but to no avail. The unicorn is too engrossed in grazing to hear the boy's call. This does not quell the boy's determination. He is eager to deliver his good news. High spirits, overwhelming enthusiasm, and drive are indicated.

DIVINATORY MEANING: This card may represent you or a person who is prominent in your life – a young, enthusiastic person under the age of twenty-five with fair hair and complexion and blue or green eyes. Rods usually depict fire signs or their characteristics: strong will, enthusiasm, spontaneity, determination. If none of this pertains to you, the alternative interpretation is that positive news is forthcoming, allowing one to actively proceed with a project or a goal.

REVERSED MEANING: The above qualities become negative if this card appears reversed. Here we find a person who is too opinionated and headstrong for their own good. A need for instant results may make this person obnoxious to live or work with. It could also be an indication of bad news.

Knight of Rods

The knight of rods portrays a gallant knight who is dynamic and bursting with energy. Mounted on a highly spirited unicorn, he enjoys the thrill of the ride, and the excitement of actually being on a unicorn. He has all the makings of an excellent warrior, and flourishes a symbol of his victorious achievement to the world.

DIVINATORY MEANING: The knight of rods is a strong-minded fire sign type who may literally rush into your life and sweep you off your feet. He is not a conformist; he prefers to do his own thing, with a devil-may-care attitude toward life. If this card doesn't represent you or a person around you, then you must look at the surrounding cards to ascertain if this dynamic card is an indication of movement and travel. If the Chariot is in the spread, travel is prominent. Take the other cards into consideration, for the message may be a change of residence.

REVERSED MEANING: Delays can be expected when this card appears reversed: delayed travel, setbacks in moving home. Be patient. You can figure out from the other cards when this frustration will lift. If the question is one of finance and the knight represents a person, there is a strong tendency for this person to be very pushy, like a salesperson going for the hard sell. Although this person may appear successful, he is not necessarily liked.

Queen of Rods

The queen of rods features a phoenix-style emblem in the top corners, as do all the royalties in the suit of rods. This is symbolic of the fire signs (Aries, Leo, or Sagittarius). The queen herself is portrayed as a dynamic and headstrong lady with flowing locks of flaming red hair. She stands tall, with a strong air of authority about her while she dictates to her subordinates. She holds her rod of strength in her right hand as a queen would hold her scepter. Marble statues of unicorns stand in the background.

DIVINATORY MEANING: This woman has all the characteristics of a fire sign. She is a strong-minded, self-sufficient
woman with a good head for business; she is a natural leader,
preferring to be left alone to get on with her work. She does
not suffer fools gladly and hates being told what to do. If the
queen of rods does not represent you or a woman in your life,
then you should let the positive characteristics of this card
come to the forefront in your own personality. You should be
encouraged to be more dynamic and assertive in your
approach.

REVERSED MEANING: The queen is too enthusiastic; she
is in danger of spreading her energies too wide and thin.
Consequently, she feels as though she is rushing round and
round in circles but doesn't feel as though she is getting anywhere. She is her own worst enemy, as her high energy level
can tend to make her high-strung. She may have a fiery temper that is liable to flare up at the slightest provocation.

King of Rods

The picture depicts the king of rods standing proudly in his
palace. He holds his rod in both hands. He is a gentleman of
substance, a strong and brave king who has fought hard to
attain his crown. He portrays all the qualities of the fire signs:
stamina, inner strength, and natural leadership abilities.
Statues of unicorns in the background of this picture depict
the spiritual strength that comes from within.

DIVINATORY MEANING: The king of rods is a mature,
genteel man of fair coloring. He is very clever and quick-
thinking; a self-made man. He does not like to accept help

QUEEN OF RODS

KING OF RODS

from others. He is forceful and determined; if he can't do things for himself, then he would rather do without. He may be a business adviser or a salesman, or he may work in advertising, because he has a flair for thinking up new ways to get a point across. As he is a very talkative person, he has many friends and gets on well with most people. Like the astrological sign of Leo, he is a born actor, versatile and able to fit into any situation.

REVERSED MEANING: When reversed, this man is still clever, but he has little patience, if any. He has a volatile temper, and makes many enemies but refuses to recognize that it is his behavior that forces people away from him. He prefers to believe that he is right and everyone else is wrong.

THE SUIT OF PENTACLES

Ace of Pentacles

The ace of pentacles shows two young unicorns leaping out from above and behind the center pentacle, indicating birth and new life. The whole scene in set in the beautiful enchanted garden of spiritual tranquility. Woodland flowers blossom as the unicorns leap for joy, for this card represents total happiness and contentment, the chance of new beginnings and fresh starts, and financial and material security. With this card, it is safe to say, the virtuous unicorn has bestowed good fortune upon you, making you spiritually prosperous as well as physically secure.

DIVINATORY MEANING: As pentacles usually relate to

financial and material matters, the ace of pentacles is a brilliant card for opportunities. If the Wheel of Fortune is next to this card, it signifies a lucky and unexpected windfall of money – maybe even winning the pools! In areas pertaining to work, this card brings opportunities for advancement, either moving on to better things or getting a promotion.

As there is always an element of risk with new ventures, you may already have an opportunity, but for some reason you are holding back. However, if surrounding cards are positive, you can afford to take that risk. Go for it! If you are looking for a loan for a new house, property, or anything that would add to your own security, now is a good time to apply for it.

REVERSED MEANING: When this ace is reversed, it brings delays and frustrations in new ventures. If you have been trying for a loan, it is more than likely you have been refused. Wait a while until situations improve and then try again. The severity of this card depends on surrounding cards. The seven of swords or Tower next to this can actually indicate loss of money, either through theft or bankruptcy.

Two of Pentacles

The two of pentacles portrays a young person juggling two pentacles in his hands. He is expressing extreme caution to avoid dropping either pentacle, as this is all he has got and thus can't afford to lose any. A young unicorn foal frolicking in the foreground appears oblivious to the serious nature of the man's predicament. This unicorn is highly spirited and just wants to have fun. Life is too short to be negative and worried all the time – so take a tip from the unicorn, and lighten up!

DIVINATORY MEANING: The two of pentacles signifies juggling finances around to make ends meet. You may be taking on extra responsibility in the near future, maybe holding down two jobs at the same time. Twos of any suit usually indicate decisions needing to be made; perhaps you're toying with which direction to take in a situation. If the Lovers, two of cups, or four of rods is next to this card, a partnership is being offered.

REVERSED MEANING: This card reversed means cutting back on work or responsibilities. You may have decided to break free from a partnership to go it alone. It is likely that a financial decision has already been made, so from looking at the other cards you can deduce if you are going to be satisfied with the outcome.

Three of Pentacles

The three of pentacles depicts a mature man working hard to build solid foundations for his future. He is a conscientious worker who looks forward to reaping the fruits of his labor. He is a "salt of the earth" type of character who believes quality counts in his work. The unicorn stands at his side, watching him build on his foundations. His positive spiritual presence gives great encouragement to this hard-working man.

DIVINATORY MEANING: This card indicates opportunities for you to use and develop your skills. It signifies craftspeople and opportunities for career advancement. In the space of three days, weeks, months, or years, you will have an opportunity to prosper financially; whether you receive a new job offer or branch out in your personal life, you will achieve success.

ACE OF PENTACLES

TWO OF PENTACLES

THREE OF PENTACLES

FOUR OF PENTACLES

REVERSED MEANING: This suggests you have become bored with your work situation and are ready for a change. You may be overqualified and in need of a more stimulating situation. A perfectionist, you tend to be too critical of yourself and others.

Four of Pentacles

The four of pentacles portrays a miserly figure, who sees all his assets as being in his sole possession. He even sees his friend the unicorn as belonging to him, as he holds him tight in his left arm. The unicorn looks as if to say "I love you, but I do not want to be possessed. I am a spiritual beast. I do not belong to anyone other than myself." In the miser's right arm, he holds a pentacle, and there is a pentacle under each foot. You could say that he appears to have everything and is secure; but he is obviously insecure, or he would not cling so hard.

DIVINATORY MEANING: Although this card portrays financial security, it may also portray the miser. Other cards need to be taken into consideration in order to determine whether the tarot is warning you to keep tight hold of the purse strings because of some threat or danger to your financial security. Or you may have a natural tendency to be overcautious with money, perhaps due to financial loss suffered in the past.

REVERSED MEANING: The tendency to be careful with money has turned into penny-pinching and stinginess. This miserly figure keeps such a tight rein on his belongings because it is probably all he has got. This person is so protective of his possessions and emotions that he opens up to no one.

Five of Pentacles

The five of pentacles portrays an artist who has dedicated her life to her spiritual calling: painting. She is painting her unicorn. This enchanted animal inspires her, bringing out the best in her artwork. Although she is obviously very talented, as it is with all artists the drawback is that this is a "feast or famine" line of business. She may receive a lot of money for this painting, but there will be no more money until the next painting is sold. Painting is all she wants to do, so she struggles on, even to the expense of her health. She cannot afford to rest.

DIVINATORY MEANING: You may feel financially frustrated, maybe as a result of loss of job or financial commitments, especially if you are self-employed and your earnings are all or nothing. If your question does not pertain to finances, then the card could indicate a feeling of rejection or failure in a relationship. If the question is of health, then you must look at the other cards in the spread to ascertain if this is a genuine or psychosomatic sickness.

REVERSED MEANING: You can look forward to a more prosperous time due to returning to work after a period of enforced rest or the economy picking up in general. You will find that you are more secure all around, both materialistically and emotionally. Health looks set for improvement also.

Six of Pentacles

A man offers the unicorn a valuable necklace made up of pentacles. He leans forward to place the gift around the beast's neck. Generosity and good fortune blossom when the spiritual unicorn smiles upon you. This necklace is full of charm, bringing security and fulfillment to those who wear it.

DIVINATORY MEANING: You may be entitled to financial assistance. If you are a student, the cards may be informing you of your entitlement to a grant; it is worth checking that you're getting everything you are entitled to. Basically the aspects look good for you now, therefore you should go for that loan, or apply for that grant; or if in business, seek out financial backing. You can't fail.

REVERSED MEANING: With the reversal of this card, we see a role reversal. Previously, you were the benefactor, but now you may be being called upon to pay back loans or other handouts. Also with this card, we see a person who may tend to be over-generous with his handouts. Take better care of your money, or you could end up with nothing.

Seven of Pentacles

A man is resting after hard labor. Both he and his unicorn look wearily at the pentacles they have already acquired, wondering how many more they need to gather before they accomplish their task. The man looks at all the hard work already done, but feels as though he has not really achieved much with only seven pentacles to show for all his effort. The unicorn is not so easily deterred, however, and will encourage the man to persevere until they reach their goal.

FIVE OF PENTACLES

SIX OF PENTACLES

SEVEN OF PENTACLES

EIGHT OF PENTACLES

DIVINATORY MEANING: When the seven of pentacles appears in your spread, you must persevere through tough times. Take into account the other cards surrounding this card; try to ascertain why you are feeling so frustrated, as if you were putting all your effort into hard work but seemingly not gaining anything in return. Perhaps you're trying to build up a new business, and you wonder if all the hard work is going to pay off. You need to carry on, particularly if the surrounding cards are indicating a positive outcome. In time, you will reap the fruits of your labor.

REVERSED MEANING: When this card appears reversed, you must be prepared for unexpected expense. This may be a rather large bill or even shaky foundations in a work environment. This is especially so if the Tower appears in the same spread. Be very security-conscious, guard all valuables, and check that all monetary transactions are correct.

Eight of Pentacles

The eight of pentacles portrays an artistic man who is busy sculpting a pentacle. With the spiritual unicorn by his side to encourage him, he cannot fail. We can see all his previous work in this picture: pentacles are proudly hung on the wall. This gentleman has all the qualities of a positive earth sign; he is a hard and conscientious worker, building up his reputation by his adamant perfectionism.

DIVINATORY MEANING: This is the work card. It indicates skills being used to their best advantage. You may be encouraged to brush up on certain skills or even turn your hand to perfecting a craft you would really like to learn.

Maybe you have an artistic streak but have always been guided away from the artistic to attain "a proper job." If you have felt frustrated with work, then maybe now is the time to turn to something new and enroll in a course at college or night school. There is nothing in this world you can't have if you want it enough.

REVERSED MEANING: It is likely that you have lost interest in your work environment. Boredom and a feeling of stagnation have taken over. Find a new interest or join a new group. What are you really like? Are you a creative person, a budding artist? Or do you have a flair for words? Bring out the more positive side of your character.

Nine of Pentacles

The nine of pentacles portrays a contented lady standing in the garden of spiritual love, quietly feeding tidbits to the unicorn. She has attained her goals and now has plenty of time to enjoy her well-earned rest. Security is plentiful with the pentacles literally growing on trees, so she has no need to worry. The unicorn has wandered into the garden, attracted by its tranquility; the tidbit he is being fed is purely an added bonus.

DIVINATORY MEANING: You are very fond of home comforts and life's little luxuries. With this card, everything looks rosy in the garden, so any home or property improvements are well aspected now and are a good investment in the long term. If this card is next to the Empress, it means fruitfulness and can indicate fertility. Security is of utmost importance; this card indicates not only financial security but also emotional security.

REVERSED MEANING: The nine of pentacles reversed is a warning of financial loss. We occasionally have to experience loss in order to appreciate gain. If the Tower, Devil, Moon, or seven of swords are next to this one, guard property matters, as there is a real danger of loss or damage to property. Depending on the rest of the cards in this spread, you may have to consider selling your house for financial reasons. Look for any legal cards or cards representing authoritative figures.

Ten of Pentacles

The ten of pentacles depicts a young couple with their arms around each other in a loving embrace. Their young child is being tended to by its grandfather. In front them is a young unicorn foal, eager to play and frolic with the child. The whole scene denotes happiness and security in the home, as three generations of family live contentedly together.

DIVINATORY MEANING: When this card appears in a spread, you are either already financially secure or on your way to being secure. It is probable that you have all the old values that enrich life, such as the family sticking together through thick and thin, and young and old sharing experiences. Providing the other cards are positive, you can enjoy peace and harmony at home. You may even be considering expanding or modernizing the family home; this will be a good move.

REVERSED MEANING: This card reversed brings severe warning about security matters. There could be trouble with an inheritance, or worse still, you may run the risk of losing your home due to financial ruin or debt. If the Wheel of

NINE OF PENTACLES

TEN OF PENTACLES

PAGE OF PENTACLES

KNIGHT OF PENTACLES

Fortune is next to this card, along with negative cards such as Death, the home may be swept away due to circumstances beyond your control, like freak weather conditions or the government running a major roadway through it.

Page of Pentacles

The page of pentacles depicts a young boy holding a pentacle up high in jubilation. The scene exudes joy and happiness, as if some excellent news has bestowed the boy with good fortune. By his side, a young foal prances around with excitement over the good news. As with all the other court cards in this suit, the pentacles represent earth signs (Taurus, Virgo, Capricorn). Thus, success will be attained by adopting a down-to-earth, steadfast approach in matters pertaining to finance or security. Therefore, the emblem for the monarchs of this suit is that of tree spirits, placed in the top corners of this card. The tree spirits twist and turn to form an archway.

DIVINATORY MEANING: Good news, successes, and attainment of goals are on the horizon. There could be some positive exam results, passing with honors. Keep in mind that pentacles usually connect themselves with financial matters, and that pages are usually messengers, so there is likely to be good news for you concerning a financial matter. If the legal cards are near this card (Justice, Judgment), expect financial news from an official source, maybe some form of compensation or money for damages.

REVERSED MEANING: When this card appears reversed in a spread, be forewarned of the possibility of disappointing news about a financial situation. It can indicate failing exams, perhaps due to the fact that you lack self-confidence. Believe in yourself and to try to overcome your insecurities.

Knight of Pentacles

The knight of pentacles sits astride his unicorn, victorious in his pose. He has returned from traveling far and wide, having experienced many great and wonderful things on his journey; but he has also become more mature. He holds a pentacle under his left arm for the lady in his life. He intends to offer her this pentacle tonight when he asks for her hand in marriage. The knight of pentacles is a handsome, debonair gentleman who thinks long and hard before entering into any form of commitment.

DIVINATORY MEANING: Linked to earth-sign qualities, this knight is a genuine, down-to-earth man between the ages of twenty-five and thirty-five. He is medium- to fair-haired with light or dark eyes. This man is very security-conscious, working very hard for everything he attains in life. If he does not represent you personally, then he could be a good friend, business associate, or suitor. He may be offering something to you, as proposals are indicated by this card.

REVERSED MEANING: When the knight of pentacles appears reversed, it is likely that you are a work-a-holic. You must lighten up a bit, because although it is rare that you ever fall ill, it is not good to be so engrossed in work all the time. You could end up running yourself into the ground. Sometimes this card appears in the spread of one whose spouse is always working, making the other feel rejected. If something is not done, the marriage will suffer.

Queen of Pentacles

The queen of pentacles is portrayed here sitting high on her throne. The young unicorn is lured by the queen's beauty and virtue. He gently places his head on her lap. The queen strokes the unicorn with one hand while holding her pentacle in the other. She is a down-to-earth, nature-loving person, but she can also be very materialistic at times. Security is important to her, but so is the love and comfort of this beautiful, spiritual beast.

DIVINATORY MEANING: The queen of cups is a self-sufficient, realistic, trustworthy lady. With earth-sign characteristics, she is very much a humanitarian but also has a good head for business. She is very wise, giving excellent advice to whomever turns to her for guidance. Listen to the advice of this trustworthy woman, for if she does not represent you, she may be a mother, sister, wife, or good friend.

REVERSED MEANING: This woman has become far too materialistic. She comes across as a false person who is only interested in what you've got and what you can do for her. She is a social climber who may be seeking to marry for money. Deep down she has serious insecurities, with a tendency to feel inferior; hence she puts on airs and graces.

King of Pentacles

The king of pentacles is on his throne, also holding his pentacle on his left knee while the unicorn places his head on the other knee. The king is a gracious and generous man, but he will not be taken advantage of or made to look a fool. Woe to anyone who dares to cross him, for he will see that justice is done.

QUEEN OF PENTACLES

KING OF PENTACLES

DIVINATORY MEANING: This man is an important person who is very experienced in the world of finance. If he does not represent you, then he is someone you should turn to for advice – particularly financial advice. He may represent your spouse; he's a hard-working, professional man, possibly in his own business or in a highly respected position with people working under him. He is loyal and dependable, but a little too aloof sometimes. In his relationship, he may have the attitude of "if I did not love you, I would not be here." He must lighten up a little and make time for fun.

REVERSED MEANING: When this card appears reversed, you must steer clear of get-rich-quick schemes. It would be more beneficial for you to put effort into planning rather than plunging into a venture that is very unlikely to pay off. Also be warned of the possibility that you are being ripped off, especially if the Magician reversed is in the spread. This card can also represent an earth sign, but when reversed the negative traits of the earth signs take over, making this king very stubborn and not willing to listen to reason. The king is also possessive, seeing everything in his life as his property, including his family.

Chapter 5

Using Tarot Cards

Some people say it is bad luck to read your own cards, but I learned to read tarot cards through practicing reading for myself, and advise you to practice as often as possible. Play with your tarot cards, take notes, look at the different pictures, and notice the order in which they spread out.

Practice the following tarot card spreads on your family and friends. This will enable you to become proficient with your cards. Do not be frightened to say what you feel, but remember to choose your words carefully. You are in a responsible position, dealing with other people's emotions.

There are many different tarot spreads, and I have chosen two for this book. The Celtic Cross is probably the most well-known spread. The Path is a very old and effective layout. Once you become familiar with the cards, you may wish to devise a spread of your own.

Advice on Counseling

When consulting the tarot for someone, this someone becomes the *inquirer*. Try not to be nervous. Deep breathing will help to relax you, clearing your mind of the day's events. First, ask the inquirer to shuffle the full tarot deck. Ask him or her to think about nothing in particular, just to silently ask the tarot to tell them if there is anything they should know for the near future. Use the instructions outlined in this chapter to guide your reading.

Please remember: you must choose your words very carefully when advising the inquirer about a problem in the cards. Do not abuse the tarot's gift and frighten the inquirer. Remember, tarot cards show the *potential* for the future. Nothing is absolutely definite with the cards. Therefore, you must inform your clients that they are masters of their own destinies; the tarot merely acts as a guide.

Time Scale

You may be asked if you can attribute times to tarot predictions. It is very difficult to get an exact time from the tarot cards alone. You must rely more on your own intuition, which will become heightened the more you practice.

Ask the inquirer to shuffle the cards, mentally asking the tarot to give an indication of time scale, then pick three cards anywhere from the pack. Sometimes you may pick up a feeling from the cards, i.e., winter scenes indicating that time of year, sunny pictures indicating summertime. The other method is as follows:

ACE = One day, week, month, or year.

PAGE = Eleven days, weeks, months, or years.

KNIGHT = Twelve days, weeks, months, or years.

QUEEN = Thirteen days, weeks, months, or years.

KING = Fourteen days, weeks, months, or years.

The rest of the Minor Arcana is self-explanatory: twos, threes, fours, etc.

THE CELTIC CROSS

When the inquirer has shuffled the cards well, then ask him to split the full deck in half with his left hand. Place the bottom half of the deck on top. Now ask him to pick ten cards from anywhere out of the pack, placing them face down in a pile on the table. Starting with the bottom card (the first to be pulled out from the pack) begin placing the cards on the table in the order shown in the diagram.

Positions and their Meanings

The first card represents the inquirer, and is placed in the center of the table.

The second card represents the situation crossing the inquirer. In other words, this card should give you an indication as to what is worrying the inquirer at the time of reading.

The third card indicates the foundation of the question. Placed below the first two cards, it indicates whether the inquirer is treading on shaky foundations or is secure in stable surroundings.

The fourth card indicates past influences that may still be affecting, or even be the cause, of the inquirer's present situation. This card is placed to the left side of cards one and two.

The fifth card crowns the inquirer. This card is placed directly above the first and second cards, indicating how the inquirer appears to the outside world.

The sixth card is placed to the right of the first and second cards, and represents near-future trends and the possible happenings yet to come that could have a bearing on this situation.

The Celtic Cross

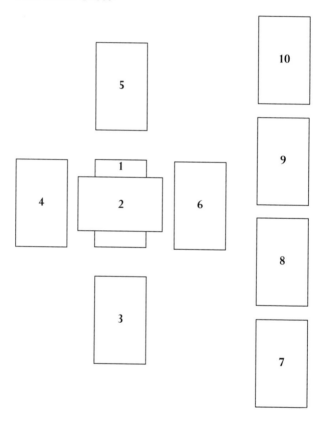

The seventh card is placed lower down, to the right hand side of the first cards. It begins the line of cards that will ascend straight up in a row on this side. The card itself portrays the subconscious feelings pertaining to this question, and how the inquirer really sees himself.

The eighth card is placed above the latter. This card pertains to the inquirer's relationship with friends, indicating jealousy or support from friendships and relationships.

The ninth card is placed above the latter. This card describes the inquirer's hopes and fears about the present situation.

The tenth card is placed above the latter. This card foretells the final outcome to the present situation.

Interpret the cards individually, but also look at the whole picture in order to clearly interpret what is going on.

Example: Lay your cards out in the following spread and see what I mean by taking surrounding cards into account in order to obtain a clearer picture.

1. Queen of Cups (Reversed). This signifies a water sign female who is inclined to be over-emotional.

2. Three of Swords. This card informs us that the emotional client feels she is faced with a dilemma.

3. The Tower. This card signifies an unstable environment and shaky foundations; sooner or later something has to give.

4. King of Swords (Reversed). This indicates a stubborn male has been causing our client some frustration. He seems to be unreasonable, and because of the Tower card being present, they are probably fighting like cat and dog.

5. Strength. To the outside world, our client appears to have everything. She gives one the impression of being cool and in control, putting on a brave face.

6. Knight of Cups. Signifies another male having a strong influence in our client's life. You can clearly see from the men, one on either side, and the three of swords caressing this emotional lady, that she is on the verge of a separation. She must choose between two people.

7. The Hermit. This card is advising us that our client should take some time out for herself. She feel that everyone and everything is working against her; a period of peace and tranquility is essential for her to replenish her energies and get her act together.

8. Four of Rods. This placing for relationships looks great. This is sometimes seen as the marriage card, and considering the outcome is the Lovers, it is safe to say that wedding bells are in the air.

9. Nine of Swords. Although the cards are beginning to look much more positive now than they did in the beginning of the spread, having this placing here indicates this lady is a little too emotional. She is letting her inner fears blow out of proportion. She may even be losing sleep over the thoughts of what she may have to face.

10. The Lovers. In the end, the outcome is brilliant. True love will blossom, obstacles will be overcome. The result is well worth the fight and upset. It is a love made in heaven; therefore, it is meant to be.

•◆• •◆• •◆•

THE PATH

The Path is an ancient gypsy spread. It reveals the inquirer's current path, taking into account recent past elements (the past always has a bearing on the future); present circumstances pertaining to health, family, friends, hopes, and fears; and concluding with the outcome to the present situation.

The inquirer is asked to shuffle the whole tarot deck. While shuffling, the inquirer should try to blank their mind of any particular thoughts. The inquirer needs to concentrate and silently ask the cards if there is anything they should know for the near future.

1 The Outer Self	**6** Health	**7** Hopes and Fears
2 The Inner Self	**5** Family	**8** Friends
3 The Future	**4** The Past	**9** Outcome

The Path

After shuffling, ask your client to place the cards on the table, face down. Then ask them to split the cards into two packs with the left hand. Take the top card from the bottom pile and place it in position number one. Then place the bottom pile on top of the top pile and ask the inquirer to pick eight cards from anywhere out of the deck without looking. Place them down in the order shown above, one at a time. The pattern of this spread is in the shape of a winding path. Remember when interpreting these cards to turn them over one at a time, and then read them all together as a general outlook for the imminent future.

1. The Outer Self. This indicates how the inquirer is viewed by the outside world. For example, a person may give the appearance of being strong and in control of his or her situation, but within, may be unsure and insecure.

2. The Inner Self. This placing will give you a clearer picture of your client's true self. For example, if the cups are placed here, we are dealing with a very emotional person. If swords, then this person is very creative and clever. If pentacles, then reasonable and loyal. If rods, the person is fiery, hot-headed, and likely to be the leader.

3. The Future. This placing pertains to future influences. I have found from personal experience that situations appearing in this particular spread will tend to occur within six to eight weeks. However, it has been known for things to happen a lot sooner.

4. The Past. This represents the past influences that may have a bearing on the present situation. For example, the two of swords would indicate some form of parting, loss, or separation, whereas the ace of pentacles would indicate a windfall.

5. Family. The family and home always have a bearing on the individual. This placing will show you if the family is supportive of the inquirer or not. It may indicate a forthcoming family celebration or bereavement. Property matters also show up here – for example, a move of home.

6. Health. This placing indicates the inquirer's health condition at the time of reading. The card in this position will help you determine if health will be good or poor. You can also determine by the remaining cards, particularly the Outer Self and Inner Self, just how ill a person might be; and whether it is a slight malady or something more serious. Don't frighten your client if a negative card turns up in this position. The Death card in this placing may indicate a birth. You must look in other areas for confirmation of what the tarot is trying to tell you. Don't jump to immediate conclusions!

7. Hopes and Fears. This will give you an insight into how your client is feeling at the present moment, if the inquirer's ideas are just pipe dreams, or if he or she is feeling depressed. If a positive card falls in this position, the inquirer may be feeling elated about something. You will be able to tell from the final cards if the inquirer's hopes or fears are founded.

8. Friends. This placing will give a clear indication as to whether or not the inquirer benefits from the help of good, reliable friends (maybe the friends need to be watched). Swords in this position usually give an indication of sharp words between you and a friend, or worse still, someone you trust stabbing you in the back. On the other hand, if the page of cups is in this position, it can indicate an invitation of some kind coming from a friend. If Strength is in this position, it indicates strength from supportive friends.

9. Outcome. This pertains to the present situation, and gives a strong indication of what the final outcome is likely to be – whether the inquirer will overcome present restrictions and frustrations, or whether a celebration is likely to be the outcome.

*May the Unicorn Tarot enlighten your life, bestowing you
with clear insight and peace as it has done for me.*

Wishing you all the success in the world.

Suzanne Star

The Creators of the Unicorn Tarot

Suzanne Star inherited her psychic gift from her grandmother, with whom she lived as a child in Southport, England. Her earliest recollection of her psychic ability was when she was only five years old. Although Suzanne intended to pursue a dancing career, a job performing in a hypnotist show convinced her that she should be using her gift of clairvoyance.

Suzanne attracted nationwide publicity when she qualified for a government grant to set up as a professional clairvoyant. This matter resulted in a debate about such grants in the House of Commons in London, whereupon it was decided that no further grants should be awarded to anyone else wishing to set up in the "psychic consultation profession" in England. In 1991, BBC-TV made a film about Suzanne's experiences, and since then she has worked on BBC Radio as a "Psychic Agony Aunt."

Liz Hilton was born in Manchester, England. When she was 18 years old, Liz won a scholarship to an art and design college, where she found she was more drawn to fantasy art – fairies, unicorns, and mystical beasts – than to design. Liz has been a professional artist for over twenty years. By invitation, her art was exhibited in the 1991 Manchester Art Exhibition, and she has also been published in the United States.

Suzanne Star was introduced to Liz Hilton in 1992, and they quickly discovered that they shared the same spiritual beliefs. Suzanne and Liz have developed the Unicorn Tarot out of a shared vision. When Suzanne explained her initial idea for the deck, Liz immediately knew exactly the vision that was needed. They have worked together ever since, getting along as soulmates as though their paths have crossed before.

The Unicorn Tarot is an invitation to participate, along with Suzanne and Liz, in the fabulous world of the elusive unicorn.